THE NEW ENTHUSIASTS

and what they are doing
to the Catholic Church

THE
NEW
ENTHUSIASTS

and what they are doing
to the Catholic Church

by
James Hitchcock

THE THOMAS MORE PRESS
Chicago, Illinois

ISBN 0-88347-130-2

Contents

Chapter 1

Enthusiasm

RONALD KNOX'S *Enthusiasm*[1] has, for thirty years, continued to fascinate students of religion. Although Msgr. Knox was not a professional historian, nor a theologian in the strict sense, he was a highly intelligent and widely read man, as well as a very good English stylist. And, while research over three decades has rendered some of his historical judgments obsolete, his view of his subject remains fresh and arresting.

It is important to notice precisely what his subject is, for *Enthusiasm* is one of those books which, by reason of its title and its reputation, many people are likely to suppose they understand even though they have not read it. The word immediately conjures up images of wildly gesticulating, screaming, moaning religious fanatics transported in a state of frenzy, or less radically, people so carried away with the appeal of certain of their beliefs that they are blind to reality.

Both things are indeed part of Knox's definition of

his subject—for example, the so-called Ranters of the seventeenth century who were genuine connoisseurs of frenzy and numerous other individuals and groups who were convinced that they had found *the* truth. However, he also includes other people under enthusiasm—like the Jansenists, for example—who are not ordinarily thought of as highly emotional, in fact are regarded as rather forbidding and cold.

Knox uses the term "enthusiasm" in a fairly precise, rather technical sense, although he also disarmingly admits in the opening lines of the book that there is really no name for what he wants to discuss and that he is employing what he disingenuously calls a "cant term." Although he does not offer a formal definition of enthusiasm, one gradually takes shape throughout the book. The key phrase, perhaps, is what in one place he calls "ultrasupernaturalism." It means so complete a reliance on direct divine inspiration that existing channels of faith are either ignored or denigrated. It involves a strong sense that one has a direct access to God and has been chosen as God's instrument. Almost always it leads to impatience with those who are seen as too cold, too timid, or too formalistic in their faith.

Knox was a convert to Catholicism from an evangelical, "low church" Anglicanism. (His father was a bishop.)[2] Although even low-church Anglicanism was largely devoid of the kinds of things Knox discusses in his book, there is nonetheless a strong sense, in this work as in others of his, of someone glad to be rising above a phenomenon which is rather scruffy and embarrassing. To say that Knox deprecated enthusiasm simply because it was ungentlemanly would be grossly unfair. For one thing, of his own deep personal piety there can be no doubt. For another, if a respectably classical kind of Christianity were all he sought, he would, like so many evangelicals before him, have simply become an Anglo-Catholic. The move to Rome had much deeper implications, some of which will be discussed later.

It would be easy to say that people of Knox's sensibility are simply embarrassed by strong emotion, but this again would be unfair. Rather disarmingly, in fact, he relates, in the foreword to the book (addressed to Evelyn Waugh), how he intended originally to make his subjects into horrible object lessons of "the dangers of illuminism" and in turn to attribute their chaotic religiosity to the initial break of "the sects" from Rome. In the process of writing it, however, something happened: ". . . the more you got to know the men, the more human did they become, for better or worse; you were more concerned to discover why they thought as they did than to prove it was wrong." (It may be safely assumed that the "you" here, while it may apply to Knox himself, certainly does not apply to the man he is addressing, although Waugh quite improbably once did plan to write a biography of Charles Wesley.)[3]

By the standards of the post-conciliar era, Knox does not seem very ecumenical. He assumes orthodox Roman Catholicism as normative. He has an air of slight amusement at the often ridiculous, sometimes chilling behavior of his subjects, as though shaking his head and murmuring, "All this was so unncessary." Despite the mild conversion experienced in writing the book, if affection tinges his portraits, it is the condescending affection of a wise old uncle for a charming but misguided nephew.

But perhaps because of this attitude, Knox's book is likely to be read a great deal longer, and enjoyed a great deal more, than most historical works embodying a self-consciously ecumenical perspective. It can be argued that ecumenism in history-writing has had deleterious consequences which outweigh the good effects. While removing certain old prejudices, it has sometimes introduced new ones. Above all, however, it sometimes has the effect of trivializing history, so that the great theological quarrels of the ages cannot be conceded their full power. Blandness covers all.[4] By contrast, Knox's book is like the work of the best kind of literary critics—Edmund Wilson or Lionel Trilling—who engage their subjects at a personal level, do not shrink from making judgments, come to their task with a point of view which gives their writing tone and direction.

The subtitle of *Enthusiasm* is "A Chapter in the History of Religion, with Special Reference to the XVII and XVIII Centuries." Knox does not take his study beyond about 1820, because by that time, he believes, its classic story was ended, although there were certainly later manifestations. He also recognizes it as a perennial story in the history of Christianity.

Knox's understanding of enthusiasm can perhaps best be grasped by noticing who and what he includes in his survey. It begins with the Corinthians to whom St. Paul wrote a rebuking letter and who seemingly were guilty, among other things, of an antinomian contempt for conventional morality. (More of antinomianism later.)

Next for Knox come the Montanists, with their extreme sense of the inspiration of the Spirit in the lives of believers, an inspiration which finally overrode all other sources of authority. (Some of the flavor of Knox's writings can be gleaned from his comment that the decision of the great second-century Christian apologist Tertullian to become a Montanist can only be appreciated if one tried to imagine the public effect of Cardinal Newman's announcing that he had joined the Salvation Army.)

The Donatists and Circumcellions of North Africa, arch-opponents of Augustine the bishop, were Christians whose sense of personal probity was so strong that they found sin, in effect, unforgivable and therefore felt constrained to separate themselves from the Catholics who seemed all too lax in readmitting the lost sheep to the flock.

Knox's chapter on medieval heresies contains the term "underworld"—in the age of faith, deviation can only be seen as eccentric and untypical. Here his chief subject is the Cathari, or Albigensians, a rather bizarre movement which seems to have been only marginally Christian. They were dualists for whom flesh and spirit were complete antipathies. Another form of medieval heresy was that represented by the movement of the Waldensians, who emphasized evangelical poverty to the extent that all those who did not practice it were suspected of not being genuine Christians.

For Knox, the Protestant Reformation was the unleashing of enthusiasm on a grand scale. Hence, without embarrassment, he devotes most of his chapter on that subject to the Anabaptists, whom other historians have tended to treat as marginal and untypical Protestants at odds with the leading Reformers as much as with the Catholic Church. For Knox, however, they were the natural outcome of the Protestant principle, a source of annoyance and embarrassment to men like Luther and Calvin only because they confronted the latter with the full implications of their own positions.

In the seventeenth century, Knox devotes most of his attention, among the Protestants, to the Quakers, as typical of a host of enthusiastic sects which swarmed throughout England during the period before and during the Puritan ascendancy. The Quakers were enthusiasts in the most pristine sense, with their belief in the direct infusion of the individual with the "inner light," and he notes them as the only major Christian body to dispense with the sacramental principle completely.

On the Catholic side he spends a good deal of time on Jansenism and Quietism. The latter qualifies as enthusiastic rather obviously—it was a spiritual movement which emphasized the presence of God in the soul to such an extent that all formal religious practice, and indeed all deliberate action of any kind, was virtually discouraged. Jansenism, a form of Catholicism with a strong emphasis on God's election of man and a rigorist morality, seems less obviously to qualify, although Knox includes it (and discusses it at some length) because of the Jansenist tendency to appeal to God directly over the heads of Church authorities.

The eighteenth century is usually thought of as a period of cold rationalism, when religion was at rather a low ebb. Knox realizes, however, that this is true mainly at the level of the intellectuals, and not always there. At the popular and semi-popular level there was a great proliferation of enthusiastic movements—the Pietists in Germany, who exalted personal religious experience above all creed or theology; the Jansenists, still active in France despite numerous checks; and above all the movement spawned (or, perhaps more accurately, brought together) by John Wesley in England, one of the great chapters in modern religious history.

To attempt to do justice to so vast a subject as Christian enthusiasm would be impossible in one volume, even a volume of nearly 600 pages, as Knox's original edition was. Inevitably there is selection. How adequate is Knox's?

Perhaps the most striking omission is Gnosticism, which receives only one brief reference from Knox, in connection with Montanism. Virtually all scholars of early Christianity have been aware for years of the extreme importance of this movement in the history of early Christianity. Older and broader than Christianity itself, it was of pagan origins but had Jewish and Christian forms. It too was primarily dualistic, sometimes with the belief in two gods ruling the universe, a god of light and a god of darkness. Its influence within Christianity is a matter of much debate.[5]

By concentrating most of his attention on the Cathari of the Middle Ages, Knox misses material, not so well known when he was writing, that would actually have strengthened his argument. Heresy was a good deal more various in those Catholic centuries than has sometimes been supposed, and groups like the Brethren of the Free Spirit would have been prime grist for Knox's mill.[6]

The pre-conciliar "triumphalist" perspective is, as already noted, evident in Knox's treatment of the Reformation, although, as also noted, it carries certain advantages. Today, most mainstream Protestants and ecumenically minded Catholics would object to Knox's efforts somehow to assimilate the radical Anabaptists to the mainstream Reformers. However, it is worth noting that, although when Knox was writing, the Anabaptists were an embarrassment to virtually everyone, their image has been rehabilitated in recent years and is taken much more seriously.

In addition, un-ecumenical though it might seem, Knox's attempt to project Anabaptist enthusiasm back onto the mainstream Protestants is at least a defensible posture, and it is arguable that in fact the full and final implications of "the Protestant principle" are only now being revealed. Martin Luther, for example, after first having enunciated certain principles of private judgment to support his rejection of ecclesiastical authority, spent a good part of the rest of his life denying the seeming application of these principles by others of whose beliefs he disapproved —those who would reform things too fast, those who preached publicly without authorization, rebellious peasants demanding social justice, Anabaptists, reformers who seemed to deny Christ's bodily presence in the Eucharist.[7]

Knox's discussion of Jansenism and Quietism is perceptive and thorough, among the best succinct treatments available. However, a lapse of thirty years does show historical perspectives changed—what seemed most obvious about Jansenists in Knox's day was their rebellious disobedience toward Church authority, hence their at least quasi-heretical tendencies. What may seem intriguing about them today is their perhaps super-orthodoxy—the determination to affirm a strict moral code and a demanding personal piety in the face of lax and permissive society.

Recent work on early Methodism tends to focus on its social and political implications (was it or was it not a nursery of radical discontent, or, conversely, of obedient passivity?), a subject which held no interest for Knox. In the end, however, he is surely correct in assuming that religious movements must be evaluated in their own terms and not as adjuncts to something else. Interestingly, Knox was one of the historians of the Wesleys to notice what recent research has confirmed—that the Anglican Church of the eighteenth century was not the spiritual wasteland it has generally assumed to have been by admirers of the Methodist movement.

Writing in 1950, it was possible for Knox to assume that enthusiasm in its classical manifestations was a waning phenomenon. The nineteenth-century examples which he deals with were sects, like the Irvingites, that had far less significance and influence than those in the earlier chapters of his book. He could not have foreseen the great proliferation of enthusiastic religious movements that has occurred since about 1970. He also had a certain blindness toward America—the few American examples he cited tend to be minor and highly eccentric. He apparently had little understanding of the persistent power of sectarian religion in certain segments of American society, and of its unashamedly enthusiastic qualities.

As noted, Knox does not give a formal definition of enthusiasm as such. However, elements of such a definition can be gleaned from his overall treatment of the phenomena:

Excessive piety. Although possibly a contradiction in terms (one might say a distorted piety, but in principle it does not seem possible to have too much of a good thing), Knox nonetheless does indicate this as one of the signs of enthusiasm. He even writes of an excess of charity, using charity not in the popular and rather sentimental sense now in vogue but in the deeper sense of love of God and through him love of neighbor. The problem comes in the desire of the individual to practice Christian virtue to a degree not attained by most other people, and to do so in a way that produces friction, division, a sense of elitism. Although Knox does not make the allusion, the parable of the pharisee and the publican obviously comes to mind.

Schism. Division within the body of the Church is the virtually inevitable result of the previous tendency. Knox goes so far as to say that "The pattern is always repeating itself, not in outline merely but in detail." Such division is inevitable because of the enthusiasts' sense of their own uniqueness and their superior piety, possibly even their sense of themselves as specially chosen instruments of God. Thus from one side they are impelled to separate themselves from those they regard as ungodly and as stumbling blocks to their own mission, while from the other side they tend to annoy more conventional Christians and become impossible afflictions to ecclesiastical authorities. They either leave the Church or get excommunicated.

For Knox, schism is itself a grave evil, and he therefore sees little good as coming from any schismatic group. Whatever good is discernible in them could have been better realized by remaining in the main body of the Church and submitting to its discipline. Thus, for Knox, the entire Protestant Reformation was tainted from the source and could not help but degenerate into bizarre and infinitely dividing sects.

Charismatic authority. Enthusiasts have an over-powering sense of the special gifts bestowed on them by God and of God's special place in their lives. While they may not begin by challenging or denying Church authority, and may (like the Jansenists) manage a fancy juggling act with regard to it, in the end they cannot concede it any final word when it contravenes, or even merely fails to support, their own special sense of mission. Repeatedly they invoke the power of the Spirit (or of some kind of inward inspiration) against ecclesiastical forms which appear dead, dry, routinized, and worldly.

Ultrasupernaturalism. This term has already been noted. By it Knox means an exceptionally strong sense of God's direct and possibly miraculous intervention in the lives of his favored ones, in such a way as to render all ordinary means of approaching him unnecessary. In Knox's view, this quality carries with it an implication of credulity rather than authentic faith. The devotee does not apply ordinary prudential skepticism to allegedly supernatural manifestations. There is also an implication of a certain pride which causes the individual to assume that everything which happens in his or her life is supernaturally caused. Putting it slightly different, Knox says such people expect more of divine grace than most Christians are inclined to do, an expectation that may flow from pride or naivete rather than profound faith.

Global pessimism. This is not Knox's term. However, it sums up his analysis of enthusiasts as people who believe grace destroys nature rather than perfecting it. Despite their frequent pride, at least ostensibly they do not take pride in their own character and achievements but in the gifts God has bestowed on them purely gratuitously. Their impatience with other Christians is frequently due to the latter's apparent reliance on human virtues and gifts, their compromises with the world.

Anti-intellectualism. This flows inevitably from the previous quality. The human intellect is seen as destroyed or totally perverted by sin. Thus it cannot really lead to truth, at least not the truth which is God. Knox was an urbane, well educated, cultured individual who spent much of his life in a university atmosphere. He also wrote in the heyday of the neo-Scholastic revival, although he was not himself conspicuously Scholastic in his modes of thinking. He had a high regard for intellect, for natural theology, for the balanced view of reality in which human and divine were harmonized. He had the classicist's sense of the way in which the critical intellect restrains, corrects, shapes, and guides spontaneous outpourings of the heart. In this light he saw enthusiasts as people who not only acted rashly and without thought but as people who trod contemptuously on centuries of careful and profound thought.

Theocracy. Because they are convinced of the indubitable rightness of their own positions, and because they believe they have been given a unique mission from God, enthusiasts tend to want to use coercive power to bring about the reign of the saints, the kingdom of God. Knox did not make use of the considerable body of writings that analyze the tendencies of messianic politics, much of which was still rather new when he wrote. However, his claim is, in effect, that enthusiasm in religion tends towards totalitarianism in politics, an impatience which demands results immediately. This particular claim of his is difficult to evaluate because so few of his enthusiasts were ever in a position to exercise this kind of power.

Millenarianism. Basic to the Christian Gospel is the belief in the Second Coming of Christ. Enthusiasts almost of necessity see themselves as living in a very special time, since they also see themselves as very special people. Since God has given them an extraordinary mission, it follows that he must intend something great, possibly Christ's Second Coming, in their lifetime or at the very least the reign of the saints which will precede that coming.

Mysticism. A weakness in Knox's book is his failure to discuss the differences between authentic and inauthentic manifestations of the things which he discusses. He naturally dwells on the enthusiasts' tendency to experience at least the trappings of mysticism—divine voices, ecstasies, visions, etc. But unimpeachably orthodox saints have experienced the same things, a fact to which Knox does little more than allude. In general, he represents the genial, civilized religious outlook of the classically educated Catholic of thirty years ago—not in the least doubting of the supernatural, but waiting for an official Church pronouncement before committing himself to any particular manifestation and, in general, regretting the emphasis placed on such factors by those apparently requiring tangible proofs for belief. Mystical expriences are regarded as inevitably tending toward a kind of subjective private sense of revelation.

Antinomianism. From the Greek "opposed to the law," this is a recurrent tendency in the history of Christianity, in which those who believe themselves to have a pure faith proclaim their liberation from the mere observance of the law which characterizes lesser people. There are two forms of antinomianism. In one form the true believer does all that the law commands, and indeed a great deal more, but does it out of love rather than duty. Obedience to the law is deemed a base motive, since it implies an unloving heart and a minimalist mentality. In the other kind of antinomianism, rarer but still sometimes met with in history, the believer's exemption from the law manifests itself through a deliberate and public flaunting of behavior forbidden to lesser creatures, in particular things having to do with sexual morality. Knox notices how often a rigorist morality accompanies enthusiasm, but he also perceptively notices how often, by strange sleight-of-hand, this is transmuted into a claim of antinomian liberation. The pride which he believes to lie at the root of the enthusiast's godliness easily leads to a grandiose self-assertiveness.

Lust for martyrdom. Since the martyr's crown is the highest culmination of the Christian life, the enthusiast naturally seeks it as a seal of his chosenness. He also regards it as natural and appropriate that he should suffer at the hands of the ungodly who surround him. Knox holds to the classical view that one should not seek martyrdom but should accept it if it becomes inevitable. (It might be suggested that at almost every point St. Thomas More is the opposite of Knox's enthusiast.)

Invisible Church. There is a quite orthodox sense in which there is an invisible church. However, for Catholicism there must, obviously, be a visible church which is the outward form of the invisible community and which cannot be thought seriously at variance with the "true" church. Enthusiastic groups, however, commonly do not recognize the importance, or indeed even the reality, of the visible church. Proceeding from their elitism, they posit a church which is a hidden community of saints. The visible church becomes at best unnecessary, and often is treated as a hindrance and an obstacle to the true faith.

Desire for results. Because they are millenarians, in the sense of expecting the imminent advent of extraordinary things, and because they believe themselves charged with particular tasks by God, enthusiasts look for immediate and tangible results. The classical Christian idea of laboring patiently in the vineyard, working routinely for a harvest which may be in the distant future, is not for them. When expected results fail to materialize, they sometimes blame themselves—their faith was weak and hence unfruitful. Often they are tempted to force results. (On occasion in history this has taken the form of violent attempts to bring the kingdom of God to birth on earth.) It may also lead to loss of faith. Having been taught to expect spectacular results, the enthusiasts easily becomes disillusioned.

Experimentalism. For the enthusiast, personal religious experience is everything. There is disinterest, sometimes even hostility, toward all forms of religion which seem impersonal. This commonly includes doctrines, rituals, ecclesiastical structures, and all other things which do not emanate directly from the experience of the individual. It can be called experimentalism in that it often involves active cultivation of religious experiences. A piety which does not issue in continually new and fresh experiences is deemed deficient, and experiences are taken as the essential test of a piety's authenticity. There is little room for the mystics' "dark night of the soul," nor even for the routine spiritual dryness which most believers experience as a matter of course. It is also the aim of enthusiastic piety to get others to have the same experiences. These are regarded as a great cache of riches which must be disseminated to those who are worthy, and the validity of all evangelization is also tested by the quality of religious experience it generates.

Knox's identification and dissection of the phenomenon of enthusiasm was a new and important contribution to the history of religions, for although many people had noticed the phenomenon before, no one else had attempted to describe it so comprehensively.

His anatomy of the movement has not been immune to criticism, and in particular he has been faulted for his almost complete lack of sympathy for what he studied. However, it is not apparent that a negative mentality disqualifies a student of a subject any more than does a friendly one. Each in its own way is likely to make the scholar sensitive to things which might otherwise elude him.

When Knox wrote there was relatively little of the thing he described, at least in respectable religious circles. Now there is a great deal. How well has his analysis held up, and how well does it explain the present religious scene? The answer to those questions is complex and leads fairly far afield from Knox's own chosen subjects.

Chapter 2

The Religious Revival

WHEN Knox wrote in 1950, the religious situation in the West seemed fairly stable, even, in fact, comfortable. Although rates of church membership, and probably belief itself, were down from the Victorian era, religion was still a strong public influence. In Knox's England, if the working classes were to a great extent "lost" to the established church (although not to the Methodists and the Catholics), the intellectuals still regarded it with some degree of seriousness—T.S. Eliot even took up the Sunday collection in his London parish. Roman Catholicism seemed indeed to be flourishing. Religious spokesmen like Knox could run the risk of seeming a bit complacent—at last we have purged ourselves of these rather scruffy manifestations of faith, he seemed to say, and what remains is solid, rational, and properly restrained. Perhaps a slight possibility of dullness was all the mainstream churches had to worry about in 1950.

This comfortable kind of religiosity ended rather

appropriately with the end of the decade. Although it was not apparent at the time, it could be dated in America almost from the election of John F. Kennedy in 1960, for although Kennedy's Catholicism was much commented on, there came to be little doubt that he was a largely secular figure and the lesson he seemed to teach was that religion was at best an expendable private eccentricity.

It was perhaps less Kennedy himself than what can be called the Kennedy spirit which accounts for the secularity of American (and indeed of Western) culture in the 1960s. In retrospect what is remembered about the era are the New Left, the hippies, and the sometimes violent repudiation of all things "establishment." But that was merely the mood of the second half of the decade. The most influential religious book of the era, Harvey Cox's *The Secular City* (1965), was quite establishmentarian. Cox celebrated pragmatism, coolness, technocracy, and political skill. His thesis was that the most important human problems were susceptible of disciplined, rational, human manipulation which rendered religion very problematical. Why pray when the solution to one's problems lay in study and work? What role could really be assigned to God in a world which seemed to operate according to quite knowable natural laws? Finally, what justification could there be for spending time in church, in theological speculation, in other-worldly pursuits, when so many pressing invitations to secular action seemed to pour in from all over?

This mood of self-confident technocracy was passing even as Cox's book appeared. It was a posthumous theology for the Kennedy years. However, it struck the mood of a generation of Christians, especially, perhaps, clergy and seminarians. It did not cause, but it provided the rationale for, an outpouring of church personnel into secular occupations, many of them giving up their religious roles entirely, others keeping them but seeking to redefine them in essentially worldly ways. For a time it was permissible, indeed even mandatory, to admit publicly that prayer, worship, spirituality were problematical things, either not viable at all or viable only if radically changed.

This new secularity coincided with a violent repudiation of the Kennedy spirit—that kind of self-confident technocracy seemed in retrospect to have been responsible for the Vietnam War and for a complacency which had failed to solve the problems of race and poverty. However, the repudiation of the Kennedy spirit did not involve a repudiation of Kennedy's essential secularity. Rather the reverse happened. The mood of the late 1960s (to which Harvey Cox had no trouble adjusting) became overwhelmingly anti-establishmentarian. The Church (all the churches) were clearly part of the establishment. Therefore religion itself was attacked with often ferocious anger, when it was not simply ignored.

The new radicalism was militantly secular. Much of it was explicitly Marxist. Even when it was not, the

Marxist notion of religion as a kind of distraction from the social struggle was widely held. Either religion had no meaning, being simply an atavistic illusion, or its meaning was pernicious—precisely to offer false consolations to the oppressed. Most people were not certified New Leftists. Perhaps a majority held the New Left in distaste. Nonetheless there is no doubt that over a decade's time the New Left did indeed pull the entire society in a leftward direction, much farther than would have been thought possible in 1960. Within the Catholic Church priests and religious served as vehicles for the dissemination of avant-garde ideas, especially among the young.

The New Left saw a rebirth of Knox's enthusiasm, but in a wholly secular context. What it saw in fact was the rebirth of something of which Knox took no notice—secular millenarianism. The dominant political mood of the period 1965-1973 was one of demanding and expecting instant social change, the instant toppling of allegedly corrupt structures, the instant appearance of humane new social forms. Although not claiming supernatural authority, the new radicals nonetheless claimed a privileged comprehension of history, an insight which enabled them both to comprehend the utter corruptness of what existed (something the complacent "silent majority" could not) and to visualize utopian alternatives. Possessed of this vision, they felt justified in hastening the demise of the old and the birth of the new, by violence if necessary. Even those who did not employ violence demanded tangible signs of imminent and radical change.

The new political utopianism collapsed for a variety of reasons, many of them internal, many of them related to the inevitable disillusionment likely to fall upon all utopians sooner or later. The presidential election of 1972, with the overwhelming repudiation of George McGovern by the electorate and their choice instead of Richard Nixon, can be taken as the symbolic end of the New Left era.

In the process a strange thing happened. The thoroughgoing secularity which Harvey Cox had first celebrated in its establishmentarian forms and which then manifested itself in radically utopian forms, suddenly began to lose force. As a practical working philosophy it perhaps continued to be the creed of a majority of people, as it may well always have been. However, public professions of the self-sufficient, technocratic, worldview became less and less respectable. Even more wondrous, public expressions of religiosity became newly respectable.

Numerous historians and sociologists have pointed to a revival of belief in magic as an accompaniment to periods of social and spiritual breakdown and the anxieties these engender. In 1960, and indeed as late as Harvey Cox's bravely technocratic technology of 1965, such a revival seemed wholly out of the realm of possibility. Belief in magic survived in the "underdeveloped" parts of the world, but wherever science and technology had ventured its credibility had been destroyed. In America, in 1960, lingering belief in magic survived only among people considered marginal to the mainstream of industrial society—usually poor, uneducated, and rural or, if not, then recognizably eccentric and even dotty. So hopelessly outmoded did magic seem that Catholic liturgical reformers of the 1960s spent much energy expunging all "magical" elements from the forms of worship—ritual gestures had to be minimized lest people mistake them for efficacious acts rather than symbols. Ideally, statues and shrines should be removed so as not to become the objects of idolatry. Some reformers thought it better to eliminate almost all ritual worship rather than run the risk of encouraging magical notions, and there was unanimity of enlightened opinion to the effect that any taint of magic which adhered to the Church would be severely damaging, so foreign were such things to the contemporary mind.

In the 1950s some newspapers published astrological horoscopes, but it was assumed that these were read mainly by elderly ladies. Suddenly, around 1970, astrology became respectable. Entertainment personalities, athletic heroes, trendy young entrepreneurs, sometimes politicians admitted publicly that they believed in the stars, that they consulted their horoscopes before undertaking action, that such powers were real and important. In some circles a professed disbelief in astrology came to seem stranger than credulity. To what extent neo-astrologism has been merely a fashionable game, a cultural affectation, is difficult to judge. But it is worth noticing a fact rarely mentioned in connection with it—belief in the power of the stars over human lives is a recurring historical phenomenon in periods of great anxiety when life seems meaningless and impervious to purposeful human action. It expresses a profound sense of unfreedom, of man's passive victimization at the hands of forces he cannot comprehend or control. Astrology provides intellectual satisfaction—it an-answers the question of what causes things—and a certain measure of emotional security, but at a cost of inducing passivity and even despair.

In 1960 historical opinion about witchcraft was roughly divided between those who thought it was purely the invention of hysterical persecutors projecting their own anxieties onto hapless victims and those who thought there were self-conceived witches who believed they possessed magical powers. Both groups agreed, however, that witch beliefs, which had largely faded out of Western culture in the late seventeenth century, were survivals of pre-scientific attitudes that had long been incredible. The claim that witchcraft was an underground cult surviving from pre-Christian times[2] was regarded as laughable. Yet, by the mid-1970's, this claim was being treated to solemn and credulous respect in the media, as women, some of whom were educated and not exactly pre-scientific in their attitudes, began to claim the status of practicing witches, at the same time accusing Christianity of having distorted the meaning of historical witchcraft, which was now defined as a wholly benign magic. Many of those who would have guffawed a few years before no longer did. In fact it became a quasi-official tenet of the feminist movement that witchcraft was an ancient female religion driven underground by a patriarchal Christianity, only to be revived in the last quarter of the second millenium A.D.

In 1974 a strange film began packing in audiences all over America. Given the aggressive secularity of the previous decade no one could have predicted that by the mid-1970s one of the apparently most persuasive themes of popular culture would be possession by the devil and the possibility of exorcism at the hands of a priest. Yet *The Exorcist* started a popular cult which, by the end of the decade, was diminished but still viable. It had spawned numerous imitations, and the supernatural had, for many people, taken on a reality that was not only serious but something of an obsession. Throughout the post-*Exorcist* period reports trickled in of exorcisms attempted in real life, of individuals reporting themselves afflicted by the devil, of satanic rituals accompanied by the shedding of animal and occasionally human blood, of "covens" and other groups of satan-worshippers. A self-declared "church of satan" even got rather serious treatment from a Dominican priest.[3]

For years it has been a truism, among literary critics for example, that evil is dramatically easier to render than good. Milton's Satan, to generations of readers, has been more plausible than his God. The 1970s saw an immense reconfirmation of that truism. People who did not seem to believe in God in anything like the traditional sense nonetheless seemed to believe quite strongly in the devil. Somehow the power of evil in the universe was real to them in a way that the power of good was not.

The same period of history saw the proliferation of innumerable cults which defied categorization—the worship of ancient pagan divinities, whether historical revivals or new inventions; rituals and vestments of new and bizarre liturgies; promises of total salvation and transformation, bought at the price of complete and unhesitating adherence to the rules of the cult.

The most famous were those which revealed a sinister aspect: The Manson Family murdered virtually at the command of a crazed and hypnotic leader; Rev. Jim Jones persuaded hundreds of followers to follow him to the jungles of Guyana, where he managed to persuade many of them also to murder at his behest and finally to commit suicide on command; not violent but nonetheless troubling was the Unification Church, under the direction of the mysterious Korean, Rev. Sun Yung Moon, which also seemed to exercise a kind of hypnotic authority over young Americans, some of them of good educations.

In the pragmatic, hyper-politicized atmosphere of the 1960s probably no creed could have seemed more remote from "relevant" concerns than Asiatic religions, especially those, like Buddhism, with a monastic component. There had always been Westerners fascinated with Eastern religions, but such fascination had been thought of as rather odd and ultimately insignificant. After 1970, however, an open interest in Eastern religions became quite fashionable, precisely in those circles which had been uncompromisingly politically minded a few years before.

The spirit of the new religiosity seems to have been faithful to authentic Asiatic religion in certain respects at least—it talked of the primacy of a spiritual realm beyond appearance and beyond the hurly-burly of daily life, the need for discipline which would enable the individual to attain inner peace, enlightenment, and detachment from the illusory and corrupting world of the senses. Suddenly all kinds of people talked knowingly about the practice of meditation, many of them people who, a few years before, would have dismissed the idea of prayer as a superstitious illusion.

"Back to nature" movements have been a recurring feature of modern history, predicated on periodic and predictable disgust with the artificiality of civilization. However, these have not usually been accompanied by religious movements. In the 1970s some of them were. The combinaton of nostalgia for nature and guilt over the historic fate of the American Indians combined to arouse in some people a renewed interest in American Indian religion, which was alleged to be close to the rhythm of the natural world, in touch with the earth, the sky, and the seasons, in contrast to the Western technological mindset, which approached nature only in a spirit of dominance and exploitation. (In the midst of this revival a strange thing happened—Christianity, which had so often been excoriated for allegedly opposing the scientific spirit of progress, was now blamed for having promoted that same spirit, because it took from the book of Genesis the belief that man has been given dominion over nature. In retrospect, apparently, it would have been better if the Church had opposed science and technology more resolutely. It was no accident, some of the avant-garde now began to insist, that the fullest development of the technological mentality came to bloom in the Christian West.)

Interest in American Indian religion actually seemed to reveal something deeper—an attitude toward nature which was virtually pantheistic, an attitude in which nature itself was venerated as sacred. Some people showed an ultra-romantic desire to allow themselves to be absorbed back into nature. Avant-garde moralists began to question whether human beings really had rights superior to those of animals. Crusades to save the environment took on religious fervor, and for many people they came to partake of a moral absolutism which was denied in other areas of life.

There is no way of succinctly summarizing the myriad movements of the 1970s which are conveniently lumped under the heading of the "human potential movement.'' However, although methods among the various movements differed considerably, they seemed to share certain common assumptions. Among them were the following: (1) That human nature is wholly good and simply lacks opportunity to realize its potential; (2) That almost all social forms and established institutions are oppressive of this potential; (3) That what is conventionally called morality is merely a ploy whereby oppressive restrictions are imposed, or else is a self-created form of oppression used by the timid as a security blanket; (4) That most human beings are trained from infancy to mistrust their own potential and require techniques and encouragement to overcome their self-restraints; (5) That among the most important of these restraints is the sense of obligation or duty to others which most people possess; (6) That the road to self-fulfillment lies in the direction of increasing degrees of self-assertiveness and repudiation of unwanted obligations; (7) That existing social relationships, such as marriages, have to be either drastically altered or dissolved in order for individuals to attain their full potential; (8) That the attainment of this potential is roughly equatable with personal desire (except in extreme cases people should seek to fulfill their desires, despite social consequences).

This ''human potential movement'' had some respectable intellectual parentage in the so-called humanistic psychologists—Erich Fromm, Carl Rogers, Abraham Maslow—who had been working to some extent in conscious opposition to the deep pessimsim of Freud. The progeny of this parentage were uncountable—encounter groups, Transactional Analysis, EST, primal scream therapy, and a host of movements concerned primarily with sexual liberation immediately come to mind. The 1970s revealed an enormous hunger for this kind of "liberation," mostly on the part of people who were affluent and well-educated. Despite its patent denial of Christian doctrine on several key points, this movement had tremendous influence in religious circles, including Catholic religious orders.[4]

Already, around 1970, an odd phenomenon was noticeable in certain large American cities and near some trendy university campuses—young people dressed in the familiar style of the radical counter-culture but, instead of publicly affronting established conventions, accosting people on the street to ask, "Are you saved?" . . . "Have you found Jesus?" These were the "Jesus freaks," at first inexplicable, so totally contrary did they run to the reigning spirit of the 1960s, but harbingers of what would be one of the major movements of the next decade.

Many of those attracted to new, often unchurched, amorphously evangelical Christian movements were precisely refugees from the New Left and the counter-culture, the last people who would have been expected to embrace an approach to life hitherto associated almost entirely with marginal people, mainly rural and uneducated. Yet, in its various forms, the evangelical movement continued to grow during the 1970s, on college campuses among other places. Prayer groups, Bible-study groups, the Campus Crusade for Christ, the Fellowship of Christian Athletes all gave testimony to the tenacity of evangelical roots in what had previously been thought of as rather stony soil. Meanwhile, it was noticed even by mainstream religious leaders that the more evangelically oriented churches were growing rapidly, as the more liberal churches stagnated or even lost membership.[5]

The greatest religious phenomenon of the 1970s was something which knowledgeable observers scarcely even noticed at the beginning of the decade—the charismatic movement. First referred to as "pentecostalism," its existence was noted but was also assumed to be exclusively the preserve of the same uneducated, largely rural people, marginal to the mainstream of society.

Catholic pentecostalism began in 1966 and by the early 1970s was spreading rapidly. Now called the charismatic movement, it made an amazingly large number of converts within Catholic ranks within a remarkably brief period of time. Its impact on other religious denominations was hardly less powerful. By 1975 it was the most formidable religious movement on the American scene and was having significant influence in other parts of the world.

Charismatic piety was quite different in tone and style from what most Catholics, Episcopalians, Lutherans, or indeed most Christians in the established churches were familiar with. What was most striking about it was the powerful and unassailable sense which its adherents had of the reality of God in their lives, of the reality of miracles, of the direct inspiration which they received from the Holy Spirit. However, these claims were evaluated, they were a striking reversal of the sometimes astringently secular kind of Christianity which had been fashionable in the 1960s.

The same could be said, in fact, about virtually all the movements whose existence has been noted here. By the mid-1970s the secularized society which had apparently been the America of the previous decade had turned into a kind of religious tropical jungle. This is not to say that thorough secularism—a kind of satisfied, incurious worldliness—was not also met with quite commonly. But the kinds of religiosity which had seemed doomed to extinction in the 1960s suddenly underwent a recovery, and, rather than the next decade's belonging to a secularized belief, it belonged to kinds of religion which no prophet of the previous age had foreseen.

There was enormous difference also among the various groups and movements discussed here. However, they all in their way betokened an intense new religiosity, and one which was altering the religious landscape of the United States perhaps beyond recognition. How can this unexpected development be accounted for?

Chapter 3

The Ecology of Belief

PERHAPS the most important and lasting development of the 1960s was one that was little noticed at the time. (The most important aspects of cultural change are rarely noticed while they are occurring.) It was the full-blown emergence of a phenomenon aptly designated "the imperial self."[1]

Superficially the 1960s were a time of altruism. In fact, one of the most serious charges leveled at the bourgeoise mainstream of society was that it was selfish and hedonistic and that established institutions sanctified that selfishness. The New Left demanded that America surrender its privileges on behalf of the poor, the oppressed, those marginal to society. Banners were raised on behalf of others besides oneself.

The degree to which 1960s' radicalism was always self-interested—anti-war activity mainly motivated by the determination not to be drafted, for example—is open to discussion. More important, however, is an underlying attitude which influenced even altruistic politics, an attitude which pitted the pure individual against a corrupt society and which therefore granted to that pure individual moral and social privileges.

New Left tactics routinely involved violation of the law, ranging from minor acts of trespass to bombings and shootings. To every objection against such acts, the reply—both from the New Left and from its older apologists—was that the law itself was corrupt, that the pure moral vision of the law-breaker was sufficient to judge when such violations were proper. In effect, the argument ran that any person who engaged in law-breaking of this kind was self-justifying. A pure spirit would not violate the law except for the best of motives.

Violation of civil law, even when this involved violence, was not the only issue, however, nor even perhaps the most important. More fundamental still was an attitude of casual contempt for all laws, civil and moral, which in any way cramped the style of the wholly free individual. Even those who did not occupy buildings, vandalize libraries, or plant bombs in laboratories nonetheless often seemed to repudiate all those moral obligations and restraints which would have rendered those things shocking and forbidden. The point about the occupation of private offices, for example, was not the physical act itself, or the fact that it was in violation of the law, but the utter contempt thereby demonstrated toward the persons whose offices they were. Personal mail was read, the premises were made unlivable, and the most egregious personal insults were relayed through the media. Such acts were meant to proclaim a liberation not only from civil laws but from all the constraints of civilized life, from all moral obligations to other people.

In timeless and predictable fashion, radical groups began to splinter and to fight with one another. This was made almost inevitable by what has been called the paranoid style of politics, a vision in which people received maximum encouragement to think of themselves as pitted against a massive oppressor, and as engaged in a struggle for survival. So deeply ingrained was the suspicion of all institutions that the institutions of radicalism itself came to be insupportable. New Left movements fragmented and fragmented again, as factions within existing groups accused one another of oppressiveness, of betraying the revolution. The political philosophy of anarchy came to have renewed appeal. (Interestingly, the origins of the feminist movement are said by some to lie in the New Left, where female radicals discovered that the men who were proclaiming liberation from oppressive structures allegedly wanted to perpetuate oppressive male-female relationships.)

The logic of 1960s' radicalism was in the direction of solipsism, the isolated individual in the midst of a hostile or uncaring world, the gradual stripping away of layer after layer of socially constructed illusion. First established institutions—government, schools, churches—were found to be oppressive, enemies of a free self. Then those institutions that had seemed intimate to the self, especially the family, were found to have the same visage—the "generation gap" widened, and alienation between parents and children came to be an expected, almost a welcome feature of life. Then the institutions of the revolution were themselves found to be oppressive. The individual took refuge in the company of a few carefully chosen kindred spirits, but even these relationships began to seem evanescent and unreliable.

The inherent selfishness of 1960s' radicalism lay not merely in its encouragement to self-gratification (at first the New Left affected a rather puritanical life style) but in its encouragement to regard the self as the primary and ultimate arbiter of reality, the creation of a world in which all meaningful and enduring ties were likely to be illusory and oppressive.

The shift was signified politically when the focus of attention changed from a real or alleged concern with the rights of others—racial minorities, inhabitants of the Third World—and turned instead to the self. Students, women, homosexuals, and a bewildering myriad of other groups now came forward to proclaim themselves as the most oppressed in society, as most deserving of liberation. The ordinary constraints of social existence were proclaimed as the chains of oppression. The habit of pitting the pure and free self against corrupt structures had become ingrained and merely reflexive.

At first the New Left and the Counter-Culture existed in easy relationship with one another. Drugs, clothing styles, personal mannerisms, all the accouterments of the latter supported the former in its

proclamations about the corruption of established institutions. Beards, blue jeans, drugs, and rock music
were political statements.

The puritanism of the original New Left had not
been an accident. Most revolutionary political movements go through a puritanical phase, and the first
great modern revolutionary—Oliver Cromwell—was
the quintessential puritan. A puritanical life-style is
associated with the discipline, the self-sacrifice, the
total dedication, even the religious fervor necessary to
a good revolutionary.

The Counter-Culture was the principal means
whereby the focus of social discontent was shifted
from the oppression of others to the oppression of
self. In the process, the nature of that oppression also
changed. It ceased to be primarily political (that was
merely taken for granted) and came to focus on forms
of alleged cultural oppression—the supposedly dead-
ening conformity imposed on people simply by the accepted conventons of social existence. Systematic affronting of proper manners, expected dress, and appropriate speech came to be the essence of radicalism.
Only when the sensibilities of the bourgeoisie had
been outraged, or when the bourgeoisie was finally
forced to abandon its attempts to maintain social
standards, could the individual feel completely free.

The degree to which the systematic repudiation of
personal relationships also flowed directly from that
same attitude has been underestimated. The "generation gap" of the 1960s was in essence the repudiation

by children of all obligations owed to parents—the child's duty, insofar as one was acknowledged, was merely to become independent, and independence was often equated with the repudiation of parental values.

The next stage was the repudiation of marital ties. At first marriage was rejected on the grounds that it was only a social convention. Where true love existed, who needed a mere piece of paper? Highly optimistic predictions were made that those who entered into extra-legal sexual liaisons would prove to have stronger and more enduring commitments to one another than those who depended on the formalities of the law. Before long, however, this pretense was dropped, as people began to admit that they entered into such relationships precisely because they wanted the opportunity of getting out of them easily, did not want to make permanent commitments. Marriage, and indeed all binding commitments between persons, was discovered as another link in the endless chain of oppressive social institutions.

The final (and predictable) stage in this development was the repudiation of parenthood. A new generation announced its unwillingness to have children, because children were inherently a restriction of the parents' freedom. A massive campaign was mounted, especially in the media, to "demythologize" motherhood.

Thus the frank selfishness of the 1970s, far from being a reversal of the alleged altruism of the 1960s, was a logical and even inevitable extension of it. The aggressiveness of the untrammeled ego lay at the root of the earlier political radicalism. In the later, post-political phase the full implications of this egoism were worked out. Rebellion against established norms had become not only a reflex but a kind of moral duty. Only in the act of iconoclasm could the individual be truly free.

The 1970s would come to be called the "me decade," something of a misnomer if by that was implied that the 1960s were truly a time of disinterested altruism, as its official rhetoric insisted. But certainly in the 1970s it was no longer necessary to claim altruistic motivation. A frank preoccupation with oneself, one's own "needs" and problems, began to replace political activity among the younger generation (and the avant-garde older generation) who had been responsible for the radical politics of the 1960s.

Ordinarily, a preoccupation with self seems to be the antithesis of religion, many of whose forms preach an ethic of unselfishness and all of which preach submission to the higher powers of the universe. However, there is a necessary sense in which religion promotes self-awareness, if not self-absorption. The religious person cannot simply live life in naive, hedonistic unreflectiveness. However dimly and inarticulately it is put, the religious person asks a fundamental "why" question—why am I alive, what is expected of me?, what is my relation to the larger universe? These were exactly the questions which during the 1960s had been declared irrelevant and distracting.

Two distinct causes may be suggested as responsible for the revival of religiosity in the 1970s. One was the respite from political activism which took place, as individuals, sometimes exhausted, sat back to take stock of their situations, tried to recover their roots, find resources to go on living. The culture suddenly gave blanket permission for people to occupy themselves with these "irrelevant" concerns.

The other cause was, in a sense, equally a self-creation. The 1970s were quite palpably a time of what might be called metaphysical anxiety, anxiousness about the very possibility of meaningful life. There was immense reliance on drugs and therapies of various kinds, as quantifiable evidence of social breakdown—suicides, divorces, abortions—rose sharply. Numerous reasons have been offered for this anxiety, including the force of technology, the threat of nuclear annihilation, and the pressures of corporate existence. But besides the fact that none of these explanations gets to the metaphysical roots of the problem, they are all unconvincing because they have been realities for a long time. Were they the root causes of social and personal breakdown, they should have had their effects at any time in the post-war period.

This anxiety was largely a self-creation, in that it stemmed primarily from the radicalism of the 1960s itself. Despite the veneers of idealism, it was impossible to look at that radicalism closely without sensing the destructive, even sometimes demonic energy, that infused it. Political causes often seemed like rationales for blindly destructive acts. The destruction of physical objects like buildings, and the imaginative obsession with violence, were less important than the spiritual iconoclasm which saw in family, nation, moral code, church, university, and practically every other existing social institution merely what was hateful and tyrannical. Some 1960s' radicals, consciously or semi-consciously, were genuine nihilists who seemed to have a need to destroy all civilized values. Most others were unthinking, swept along by the high emotion of their movement, heedless and insensitive about the effects of their actions.

In a sense, the gamble of the 1960s was that values could be retained even as the institutions which embodied those values were destroyed. The gamble was by and large lost, if, indeed, many of those who played with the dice did not in some part of their being hope for the thrill of losing, of watching everything being swept away.

The 1970s was not the wholly free, institutionless world which the previous decade's radicalism had promised. All the assaulted institutions still stood, battered but functioning. However, they had lost much of their moral authority, a loss largely attributable to their patent spiritual weaknesses displayed during the 1960s. When the legitimacy of nation, church, family, and school was denied, and sometimes their very existence symbolically negated, those who had responsibilities as statesmen, clergy, parents, and educators frequently responded with signs of bewilderment, fear, masochistic self-criticism, and abandonment of authority. Those who did not often seemed to sink into timid passivity.

The result was that life in the 1970s often seemed like dwelling in a ghost town—the structures still stood, but all the life seemed to have gone out of them. They barely kept out the wind, but the cold seeped in everywhere.

If it is assumed that human beings need structures, that values cannot be preserved without them, then the cultural situation of the 1970s was highly troubling. Statesmen presided over what often seemed like disintegrating societies, not believing even in their own policies. Clergy preached a studiously ambiguous gospel, reluctant to commit themselves to any creed. Parents treated their children with a mixture of neglect and principled permissiveness. Educators no longer seemed to know what they should teach and settled for teaching anything for which there appeared to be a demand.

Whether it is interpreted as the dangers of genuine freedom or the bitter fruits of a prideful and heedless profligacy, this situation was spiritually threatening. The master vice of the age was a kind of solipsism, the inability to make meaningful contact with other beings, a recurring fear of being totally alone in the universe. For many, the existence of other people was unreal. One's own needs and one's own perspective on the world alone were conceded any validity. All social relationships were treated as threatening intrusions on the self.

The spiritual disorders of the past twenty years have two distinct causes—what might be called the optimistic and the pessimistic, although the two are ultimately related. The optimistic is the sense which has been imbued in people of limitless possibilities, of a world without restraints, boundaries, or limits of any kind. Its watchword is "fulfillment," something taken to be an endless process. The pessimistic is the sense of anxiety alluded to before, the fear of a meaningless universe. The latter, however, is the inevitable result of the former, once it has resulted in disillusionment.

Although the fact of widespread drug use has been endlessly discussed, its significance has not been sufficiently noticed. Drugs are taken to relieve anxieties and to escape from intolerable situations. However, more and more in the past two decades they have been taken for largely experimental or adventurous purposes. What the latter uses have in common with the former is that all of them involve the attempt to abolish boundaries, to annihilate all forms of particularity and finitude which the individual experiences. Drugs seemed to promise total liberation from all confining identities, the fullest experience of the self as virtually infinite.

As such they are a metaphor for the dominant cultural aspirations of the same recent era. Respectable opinion, even among many people who did not themselves use drugs and who might have instinctive reservations about them, more and more came to defend the so-called drug culture. Drug-users were seen to be making an important "statement," and many non-users sensed that the suppression of the drug culture would mark a restraining trend in society that they would find unpalatable in other ways. The same was true of rock music.

However, as it turned out, sexuality came to be the principal vehicle through which the limitless possibilities of freedom were asserted. Originally sexuality had relatively little to do with the would-be revolutionaries of the 1960s. However, casual sex quickly became a feature of radical social circles if for no other reason than that their members lived under undisciplined and unmonitored circumstances. Before long, however, iconoclastic sexual behavior was itself seen as a political statement, traditional sexual restraints one more manifestation of the oppressiveness of the establishment. Elaborate theories were developed to show how sexual repression was at the root of "fascist" behavior.

Liberal moralists of the 1960s (including some clergy) were prepared to justify sex outside marriage somewhat cautiously. Generally they thought extra-marital sex required the element of love and caring to be morally permissible. It could never be merely casual or hedonistic. Above all, the participants had to be "responsible" for the full consequences of their actions.

Such advice, considered quite daring in the late 1960s, within ten years' time had come to seem rather quaint. The point of the sexual revolution which took place after about 1965 was precisely to sever sex from caring or from responsibility. What it aimed at was the legitimation of casual, recreational sex, and whatever means were found necessary to achieve this (for example, abortion) were employed. Massive propaganda campaigns, abetted by sympathetic journalists, were mounted through the mass media to eliminate all vestiges of an ethic of restraint with respect to sexuality. By the end of the 1970s the virtues of incest were being somewhat cautiously discussed by respectable psychologists.

The sexual revolution had significance on several different levels. It was a systematic assault on one of the remaining fortresses of social convention. It was a further way of affronting respectable opinion (although respectable opinion began moving rather rapidly in favor of the new permissiveness). It promised the possibility of a kind of mystical redemption through orgiastic experience—a major industry suddenly sprang up dedicated to helping people achieve the best possible sexual experiences, the failure of which was deemed a major tragedy and deprivation. Sexual adventuring was interpreted as an important means whereby restricted personalities could break out of their spiritual prisons. Above all, the sexual revolution was a premier assertion of the ego. Hitherto forbidden sexual behavior became the favored symbolic way of asserting one's total rejection of externally imposed standards of behavior, including moral ones. Hedonism was an appropriate philosophy of life because personal desire was now regarded as the only valid criterion of proper behavior, the only ultimate guarantee of genuine freedom.

The dominant cultural mood (dominant at least among a minority of influential "trend-setters") was nothing less than a new incarnation of the temptation which has been a recurring feature of human history—a temptation which has been variously referred to as promethean or faustian, and which is perhaps the original of human temptations, the one described in the Garden of Eden. It is nothing less than the positing of an infinite self, a self which is divine, which encompasses the whole universe within itself. Such a temptation sometimes issues in a religion of pantheism. It is impossible for it to issue in genuine Christianity, although it sometimes allies itself with various counterfeit forms of Christianity.

The negative source of the self-preoccupation of the 1970s was the inevitable hollowness which such grandiose dreams finally revealed. In that sense, the negative and the positive were essentially the same, although that fact was often not apparent because some people were still in the positive phase while others had passed into the negative phase. Thus it was possible, although nothing could have been more misleading, to see the self-preoccupation of the 1970s as marking somehow a betrayal of the political activism of the 1960s, whereas the former was in fact merely the inevitable working out of all the implications of the latter.

The spirit of the 1960s urged people to live without structures of any kind—political, familial, social, religious, moral, educational. Structures were posited as oppressions of the free self, mere obstacles to the self's realization of its true freedom. A kind of political, social, even moral anarchy was proposed as proper.

At first, community was proposed as the alternative to structure, but before long community began to seem merely like another kind of structure, another form of oppression. (Thus the significance of the rejection of marital and familial responsibilities cannot be underestimated.) What was left was the isolated self. The ultimately self-contradictory nature of the prevailing ideology was revealed—officially it encouraged people to think of themselves as needing no outside "interference" in their lives, an interference which soon came to be equated with all entangling personal alliances. Yet this very notion of freedom proved to be sterile and self-destructive, reinforcing the very sense of isolation and helplessness which it was supposed to overcome

For some the proclamation of liberation from all constraints was exhilarating, and the exhilaration lasted a long time (often, to be sure, kept alive by artificial stimulus). For others the crash occurred rather soon. One of the paradoxes of the Counter-Culture, only rather evasively alluded to by older observers, was the fact that the "meaningful" existence which it supposedly brought was accompanied by an undeniably growing phenomenon of drug abuse, alcoholism, suicide, mental breakdown, and simple depression. Yet the official ideology permitted no correction of this condition, in fact prevented correction by continuing to propose an ideal of human existence which systematically excluded all those social and communal supports which the human race has historically found essential to its survival.

The therapeutic self-preoccupation of the 1970s itself resulted from the same double causality. On one level it was a hopeful thing, a means whereby people were to discover how to overcome the limitations on their free self-fulfillment. It was for this that they flocked to encounter groups, to weekend workshops, to therapeutic resorts like Essalen, and it was through these, often, that they found the means to extricate themselves from marriages and other constricting relationships. On the other hand, resort to therapeutic help—both of traditional and innovative kinds—was often a desperate ploy which followed the apparent breakdown of meaning in the lives of individuals. The rhetoric of hope sometimes covered the reality of despair, and the means used to kindle hope sometimes had the effect of snuffing out the last vestiges of meaning in certain lives—people who desperately needed more structure, for example, who could have led contented and productive lives under such conditions, were instead encouraged to throw over whatever remaining structure they still possessed, to gamble their happiness on the prospect of an illusory self-liberation from all limitations.

The most obviously pathological results of this—the suicides, the divorces, the drug use, etc.—attracted attention. Usually overlooked was the way in which virtually everyone in the 1970s was affected to greater or less degree. No values could any longer be taken for granted; all were subject to sudden revision and repudiation. Marriages were no longer assumed to be permanent but rather the opposite—those which remained intact were the subject of comment. The imparting of values to children came to be a perilous enterprise, thwarted and made difficult by a hundred outside influences working against the conscientious parent. Religion more often than not became a point of uncertainty, even of contention, a source of doubt rather than comfort. People whose personal values remained fundamentally intact nonetheless reconciled themselves to a life which was spiritually much more precarious than they had previously assumed.

The relationship of all this to politics was only approximate. Politics, in the Kennedy years, had been the principal means whereby the imagination had been stirred, dreams of limitless fulfillment forged. The radical politics of the later 1960s followed from this almost naturally. However, by 1970 many of those wafted along by this expanding balloon came to realize that politics had never been their main interest, had functioned rather almost as a metaphor for the liberation of the self. They became in a sense apolitical, although the Counter-Culture sought to transform society as thoroughly as the New Left had ever tried to do.

Thus the election of Richard Nixon in 1968, and his reelection in 1972, did not signal the end of the radical era, as was often proclaimed at the time. Rather the election of Nixon served as an excuse for the overt privatization of energies, something which had been going on anyway but could now be justified on the grounds that political activity was no longer feasible. Thus the anomaly whereby Richard Nixon presided over the psychic explosion of the early 1970s. The Watergate scandal merely served to deprive his administration of legitimacy and deepen the fashionable preoccupation with self-probing as an alternative to meaningful public activity.

Much of the cultural mood of the 1970s remained

frankly irreligious. However, it was dominantly metaphysical, even when irreligious, in the sense that it was no longer considered sufficient to take life as society presented it, to perform one's chosen or given tasks in the great struggle to make a better world. In one important sense the decade aspired to be more radical than the one which preceded it—whereas the radicals of the 1960s questioned what form politics should take, in the 1970s many people who did not even think of themselves as radical were questioning politics itself. They were metaphysical in the sense that they believed that reality was not all apparent to the naked eye, was indeed subtle, convoluted, mysterious. Much of what passed for meaningful action, even on behalf of impeccable political causes, was viewed as illusory, based on views of reality which were technological, materialistic, shallow, and (the ultimate negative epithet) Western.

Life could once again be viewed as problematic, after a period (roughly the 1950s) when social values had been viewed as essentially self-validating and another period (roughly the 1960s) when the reshaping of social forms had seemed equally self-validating. On one level life could once again be viewed as problematical, that is, there were no self-evident values or self-evident paths of meaningful action. On a deeper level life was even viewed as mysterious, in the sense in which Gabriel Marcel had distinguished "problem" and "mystery," although it is a safe bet that few citizens of the 1970s knew who Marcel was.

Both the "optimistic" and the "pessimistic" currents of the 1970s fed this metaphysical interest, this passion to know what lay behind the often bewildering and treacherous appearances of reality. For those who regarded the self as an infinitely expanding and infinitely expandable force, and every apparent objective reality an intrusion on that self, the universe was necessarily seen as vaster, fraught with infinitely more complex and exotic possibilities, than conventional imagination could conceive.

On the other hand, those whose systematic repudiation of all tradition, all structure, all community, had left them bereft and often despairing experienced a kind of hysterical need to know if life indeed held something more. All inherited values having been exhausted, were other values accessible, perhaps in re-remote and unlikely places?

The election of Richard Nixon, and the supposed repudiation of the spirit of the 1960s which this symbolized, might have been thought a prelude to a revival of church attendance and formal and conventional Christianity. Such an event never took place, or at least not in the places where it was looked for—in the "mainstream" Christian denominations. Such churches continued either to lose membership or to stagnate, seemingly plagued by leakage at both ends. Many of their more conservative members withdrew because of the perceived radicalization of the churches, both theologically and socially. Meanwhile many liberal members, especially among the young, simply found religion no longer relevant to their lives, no matter how liberalized. The condition of the mainline churches was, if anything, worse in the 1970s than it had been in the 1960s.

The prevailing cultural mood of the 1970s made this virtually inevitable. For if there was a new search for meaning, a new openness to religious possibilities, the churches, after all, where the place from which many of the searchers had originally started out. They were, in a sense, the last place where the elusive meaning of life was likely to lie concealed. Formal and active church membership in the 1970s was, even among religious liberals, almost a declaration of a certain kind of cultural conservatism, a statement that one had not joined wholeheartedly in the cultural explosion of the previous decade. Even those churches which were conspicuously modernized—with psychedelic liturgies, rewritten creeds, openness to deviant kinds of people, political involvement—were suspected of purveying simply a watered-down version of the same product, now packaged more attractively but unlikely to satisfy. One of the cruelest blows dealt by fate in the 1970s was to avant-garde clergy. After having invested so much effort and energy in updating their faith to reach a new kind of audience, they discovered that the religious revival, when it came, passed them by. They were left with brightly painted and sometimes expensive scenery, but no dramatic production that anyone appeared to want to see.

Again, the religious revival of the 1970s took the forms that it did because of both the optimistic and the pessimistic currents of the culture. With reference to the first, there occurred what might be called the emergence of religious epicureanism. Hedonistic, materialistic, prosperous Americans began to discover what the ancient Epicureans had regarded as virtually self-evident—that material consumption and gratification are not ultimately satisfying. There are subtler, spiritual dimensions of life which must not be ignored.

Harvey Cox published a new book[2] which was the manifesto of the new religious epicureanism—people should cultivate the satisfactions of the spirit just as assiduously as they cultivate the satisfactions of the flesh. To reject all religion is short-sighted and self-defeating, because religion, in its vast historical treasure troves, holds many resources of exquisite beauty and delectability. The only caveat is that none of these treasures should be accepted simply in the way in which each historical religion presents them. The essential trick is in taking from each religion whatever one wants, and using it in whatever manner one wants. Even many people who did not read Cox's new book caught the spirit of the new age.

Those who had dismissed religion as an illusion in the 1960s now began to dismiss religious believers as hopelessly unimaginative and literal-minded. St. Christopher medals, icons, rosaries, ceremonial incense, statues of the Buddha, Tibetan prayer wheels all came to be accepted as valid in their own way, provided one knew how to take them. The mistake was in taking them as simple believers took them, and especially in assuming that a commitment to one set of symbols required precisely that—a commitment. Instead one could range over the storehouses of the world's religions with the abandon of a shopper in a department store with limitless credit.

The 1960s mind, it was now implicitly conceded, had been narrow and unimaginative in seeking to deny the reality of the religious dimension of existence. Obviously, so many great spiritual masters had spoken and written about transcendental realities, so many powerful symbols had been generated, so many vast religious movements had come into being that it would be foolish to deny reality to all these things. As the infinitely expanding self began to move through the vast space of the universe in search of its own fulfillment, it would inevitably travel many of the paths marked out by the great religions. Indeed, the process could probably be hastened and rendered more efficient precisely by seeking out such paths. However, all this vast religious symbolism was to be taken as exactly that—symbolism. It was not to be conceded objective existence. It was instead a metaphor for the soul's encounter with the universe, part of the process of infinite self-realization.

Much of the apparent religious revival of the 1970s was therefore illusory as far as genuine religion was concerned, for it lacked what is perhaps most basic to such religion—commitment, humble submission to what are perceived as the higher powers of the universe. Were those who shaved their heads, put on saffron robes, begged on street corners, and foreswore all meat and sex really devotees of some Indian cult, or were they half-consciously participating in an elaborate charade, a performance that for a time coincided with some felt psychic need in their lives? It is doubtful if they themselves knew for sure. Did those who put icons on their walls and wore rosaries around their necks truly believe in the intercessory powers of the Blessed Virgin? Almost certainly they did not. One could live riotously one year, puritanically the next, as an unbelieving technocrat during the winter season and a worshipper of American Indian spirits during the summer. None of this made any ultimate and profound difference, since all of it was dictated by, and predicated on, whatever ''needs'' the self experienced at any given moment. Religion was found to be too delicious to leave to the religious.

Quite predictably, Christianity did not fare particularly well in this atmosphere. For one thing it was the most familiar of all faiths. Most people undergoing the experience of ''consciousness-expansion'' had at one time started out in a church, and they had little desire to experience what their mindset could only regard as regression. Christian churches loomed up on almost every block—what treasures could they possibly offer which would not have been discovered long ago if they were real? The mystical currents of historic Christianity, because they were more neglected than other aspects of the faith, held a certain attraction, and mystical and pseudo-mystical Christian writings began to enjoy something of a vogue. However, the farther the mystic could be located away from Christianity—in Asia, for example—the more attractive he became. Many devotees of mysticism were unaware that Christianity even possessed a mystical tradition, or else were convinced that it was inherently inferior to that of the East.

Organized Christianity remained under attack in the 1970s for several reasons. For one thing, it was part of the whole nexus of established institutions which had been discredited in the 1960s, and whatever direction the Counter-Culture took it was not backwards. For another, Christianity, so often in the past accused of irrationalism and obscurantism and of thwarting the scientific world-view, was now accused of being part and parcel of the rationalism and technocracy of the West. Whatever authentic spiritual insights the religion possessed were said to be smothered under systems, creeds, codes of law, and other corrupt and merely carnal inventions. One had to reject Christianity in order to discover real religion somewhere else. Only then, perhaps, could the remnants of Christianity still be found in a few traces in its own domain. Finally, the infinitely expanding self must of necessity be culturally cosmopolitan. Whatever might be said for Christianity, it was after all the product of one's own culture. To remain a Christian was to doom oneself to provinciality, to shrink from the great adventure of soul which was beckoning. (It is indicative of the degree of seriousness that prevailed in this atmosphere that few people indeed, despite often proclaimed declarations of passionate interest in Eastern religions, showed any willingness to undertake the long years of linguistic and textual studies which would have alone been sufficient to make an adequate beginning of such an enterprise. Catholic monastic communities were not immune from the temptation of announcing their newly acquired intimacy with zen meditation, for example, on the basis of a few lectures by a certified expert or through reading a few textbook introductions.)

From the pessimistic side, the religious revival of the 1970s had a mark of desperation about it—seekers flocked to religious movements which promised meaning precisely because they had become belatedly aware that they had exhausted all the sources of meaning in their lives, that they were living at or close to a kind of nihilism. Frequently enough they did not understand the role which their own egotism had played in the destruction of values and continued to regard this nihilism as somehow the result of "society's" failures. But the results were the same either way. If some people flocked to cults in a high sense of adventure, the rolling back of yet one more barrier to expanding consciousness, others came to them in a sense of desperation. The more authoritarian the cult—Rev. Moon's Unification Church, for example, or Rev. Jim Jones' People's Temple—the better it served its purpose. Like the spiritual adventure-seekers, the desperate seekers after truth were unlikely to turn back to any Christianity they might once have known, and for similar reasons. Among the desperate, however, there was also an additional reason—conventional Christianity, after a decade of pursuing an illusive "relevance," seemed altogether too pale, too weak, too unsure of itself to play the strong role which exhausted egos now required from a faith.

Almost unnoticed amidst the more exotic and highly publicized growths, however, there were also forms of Christian revivalism springing up in the 1970s, growths whose full stature and importance would not gain adequate public recognition until nearly the end of the decade. Belatedly did the news media recognize, for example, that perhaps the biggest religious story of the 1970s had been the growth of what was broadly called evangelical Protestantism, a phenomenon whose importance was mainly recognized because of its apparent political impact prior to the 1980 elections.

Meanwhile, there had also been occurring what might be considered a sub-species of this evangelical revival, but a sub-species whose influence extended far beyond the usual domains of evangelicalism. What had been called pentecostalism, and what now came to be known as the charismatic movement, had been around since the turn of the century but had been largely confined to rather eccentric Protestant sects, not respectable on the mainline and regarded as somewhat laughable, if alluded to at all. By 1970 this piety had penetrated almost every major American Christian denomination. Countless thousands flocked to the charismatic banner, many of them from highly unlikely personal and denominational backgrounds. For a time, at least, it looked almost as though the entire Christian world in America, for better or worse, would be swept by the charismatic tide.

At the standpoint of 1970, Harvey Cox's initial thesis—that concerning the secular city and the necessary secularization of Christianity—still looked as though it might be correct. Christianity was visibly in decline, and whatever of it survived would perhaps be of the self-consciously modernized variety. The evangelical revival and the charismatic upsurge put this fond liberal illusion to rest before the new decade was many years old, however. If anything, both seemed to show that the future of Christianity lay with those forms of piety which were, in certain visible ways, old-fashioned.

The new Christian evangelicalism shared one thing in common with some of the other forms of 1970s' religiosity with which it otherwise had little in common—practically all of this new religiosity was highly expressive, that is, it seemed to rest upon and grow out of the personal religious experience of the devotee, and it permitted and indeed encouraged the free expression of that personal experience. No religion, seemingly, would have credibility unless it was deeply felt in a palpable and emotional way, and unless it could be conveyed to others in a similar way. Strong personal feeling now came to be a badge of religious authenticity, almost self-validating. In the 1970s one word seemed to predominate and control amidst the confusing welter of those things which called themselves religious. That word was "experience." Whatever else a religion had to be, it had to be at least that.

Chapter 4

The Death of Community

CULTURAL moods are often very elusive, their apparent public manifestations sometimes quite misleading. This is as true of religious moods as of any other kind.

Superficially, the Christianity of the period after 1960 would have to be pronounced as happy and optimistic. The key term perhaps was "possibility." A religion heavy with "thou shalt nots" seemed to be giving its adherent permission for all sorts of previously forbidden things. The very notion of sin—so negative and burdensome—was cosmetically redefined when it was not conveniently forgotten altogether. Liturgy struggled gallantly to reflect only light, joy, and hope, in a word to "celebrate," as a hedonistic society understood that word. Large parts of the Church, in particular certain religious communities, learned to accept the developing secular notion of "human potential," a potential which was indeed taken to be practically infinite.

This was how the "new church" often appeared to the outsider, and the way in which it is was often presented in the media. (Thus the quintessential conflict was between a smiling, guitar-strumming young nun in brightly fashionable lay clothes and a sour-faced elderly bishop in whom the juices of life had long ago dried up.) Yet a closer familiarity with the actual religious scene could not help but reveal striking evidence of a different kind of spirit. The type of worshipping communities which made "happy" liturgies a required sign of their theology were not uncommonly characterized by a good deal of acrimony (often directed at the "official church" and its representatives), restlessness and drift, intellectual and personal anxieties, and instability. Those religious communities which presented to the world a face of having achieved notable and remarkably successful "renewal" were soon discovered to be wracked by conflict, suffering abnormal membership loss, and attracting very few novices. Above all, the officially optimistic "renewal-minded" Catholics of the post-conciliar period demonstrated a remarkable pattern of instability and inability to sustain meaningful personal commitment. In the rapidly moving world of post-1960 Catholicism, the typical "Vatican II Catholic" moved through a whole series of enthusiasms, causes, movements, panaceas—each one proclaimed to be the ultimate meaning of renewal, each one in time paling, becoming flaccid and boring, sometimes even hateful. Some of those who entered most enthusiastically into the whole process of religious change ended disillusioned and exhausted, often divorced from the life of the Church completely, sometimes situated on its outer perimeter, engaged in a seemingly eternal love-hate struggle with the religion of their youth.

The movement within the Church paralleled almost exactly the movement in secular society generated by the New Left and the Counter-Culture. Superficially the Counter-Culture, too, proclaimed that life was joyous and free, and here also a direct acquaintance with the phenomenon revealed to what degree it was ridden by obsessions, conflicts, and anxieties. In both cases it was found psychologically necessary to posit an exterior enemy who was the cause of one's failure to achieve the promised level of happiness. For the secular rebel, the amorphous "establishment" served this purpose, invoked in certain particular incarnations as this seemed appropriate. In Catholicism the myth was forged that somehow the leadership of the Church had betrayed the Second Vatican Council, thus frustrating the hopes of its most ardent partisans. In both instances people who prided themselves on a certain degree of intellectual sophistication about society could not apply that sophistication to an understanding of their own experiences.

Part of that inability was their profound ambivalence about how much their own freedom was involved in what occurred. Officially their rhetoric posited an almost unlimited degree of freedom,

Church structures amenable to almost endless reshaping at the hands of intelligent and idealistic humans. However, every failure was blamed on forces beyond their own control, often on ignorant or malevolent hierarchs deliberately thwarting well-meaning reform. Although reform-minded Catholics of the 1960s were keenly aware of parallels between their own adventures and those of the secular society (they never ceased calling themselves the "Kennedy generation," for example), they never got to the point of asking why the disasters which befell well-meant reforms of the Church seemed so similar to the disasters which were befalling equally well-meant secular movements.

In some ways the most penetrating analysis of what happened to the Catholic Church during the 1960s was made, almost as an aside, by the British anthropologist Mary Douglas. Her work, although often abstruse and difficult, is profound, and its implications can be taken beyond the rather modest limits which she gave it.[1]

Ronald Knox could take hierarchical, ritualistic, dogmatic religion virtually for granted. It was normative, the standard by which the deviations of "enthusiasm" could be measured. At the time he wrote, around 1950, it would not have seemed very plausible to proclaim Catholic worship as "meaningless ritual." Those who were attracted to the Church were more often than not attracted precisely because of that ritual, and there were many who expressed admiration for it while admitting that they simply could not accept the teachings which lay behind it.

By the 1960s, however, the adjective "meaningless" had become almost grafted on to the noun "ritual." The oddity was that Catholic ritual was being proclaimed meaningless not by critics outside the Church but by active Catholics themselves, and not uncommonly by liturgists whose specialty was the study of that ritual.[2] Although the Church was attacked at many points in the 1960s, at no point was the assault more unyielding and more bitter than over the matter of worship, and the styles in which it should be carried out.

Mary Douglas has pointed out that ritual activity is primarily a heightened sensitivity to symbolism. Hence anti-ritualism derives from a corresponding weakening of that symbolism. What is presented to the world (and to the self) as a brave act of liberation is often an admission of a diminished perception of reality. What had once been full of meaning has now become opaque and meaningless.

Douglas also finds a strong sense of ritual coexisting with a strong sense of sin, in the sense of disobedience to God and to God's law. Correspondingly, the weakening of the sense of ritual is accompanied by a weakening of the sense of sin. It also tends to be accompanied by a heightening of ethical awareness—a more acute sensitivity to the ethical uncertainties and ambiguities of life, and of the need to resolve these in some conscious fashion. Moral duty and obligation are less self-evident than formerly. Much emphasis is placed on the virtue of sincerity —the condition of that person who has expanded sufficient energy on the understanding of self and the self's relation to the universe and who has made that relationship so conscious as to take account of all hidden interests, rationalizations, and evasions. Replacing the traditional moral hero admired for having done his duty is the moral virtuoso who strives, whatever he does, at least to be "honest."

Douglas postulates three stages through which a religious community might pass in its evolution. In the first, which might be called primitive, God is known by his attributes (powerful, just, etc.), belief is largely implicit, worship is fixed ritual, and sin consists in formal acts. In the second, which probably describes Roman Catholicism through most of its history, all the characteristics remain the same, except that belief and theology become explicit. In a third stage, devotees seek personal knowledge of God, discriminating theology is abandoned, worship becomes spontaneous and non-ritualistic, and sin is defined as the wrong kind of attitude.

Sometime in the 1960s Catholicism passed from the second to the third of these stages, although the roots of the transformation undoubtedly predated the era of the change itself.

Douglas links this religious-culture change to social changes which precede it, so that the first is essentially a function of the latter. Social change is likely to induce anti-ritualist attitudes, for example, because change calls into question the legitimacy of everything which is fixed. The stability of attitudes which is implied in ritual comes to seem almost an effrontery as everything in the world around it appears to be in flux. (On the other hand, historical Catholicism has often presented itself precisely as a rock of stability in a world of change.) Tightly knit social groups tend to generate stable, ritualistic religious, loose ones something like the opposite.

Such groups have a strong sense of boundaries, which Douglas also links directly to the more stable kind of religion. Positing a kind of semi-conscious analogy by the mind, she sees the ego's sense of its own serene belonging to a well-defined social group as determining its sense of its relationship to the larger universe, to God, and to the community of believers. Ritual worship according to a fixed pattern, legally defined moral obligations, a visible church body—all of these seem profoundly right to the inhabitant of a fixed and stable social world.

By contrast, a confused society also has a confused idea of God. Religious and moral duties seem problematical, even possibly illusory. A secular society is likely to be one with weak and fluid boundaries, the self-evident rightness of nothing altogether secure.

A corollary of this is the strength of the assertive

ego in a weak, ill-defined society, an assertiveness which fits well with secularization in that it encourages the attitude of detachment, skepticism, even of defiance towards God which makes unbelief possible. On another level, however, egotism in an unstable, ill-defined society is inevitable simply because the self finds little which is objective that it can fall back on. It feels left to its own resources, which must be tested aggressively.

Douglas also links the emergence of basic attitudes to reality with child-raising practices and attitudes to the human body. The loosely defined society is one in which the individual has only a loose sense of relationship to his own body, and of the individual's integration into the social whole. What is called permissive child-raising consists in leaving ambiguous the child's relationship to society at many crucial points, which thus induces a certain sense of alienation and also of possibility. The symbolism of bodily control tends to be particularly important here, and the weakly defined society sometimes manifests itself through individuals who are slovenly about their personal appearance, for example, exerting weak bodily controls on themselves. Sexual promiscuity sometimes characterizes such people, and weakly defined societies are likely to be those in which women play prominent public roles, either legally or illegally (as, for example, in witchcraft).

How far Douglas' theories (which have been elaborated and expanded here) go toward explaining contemporary religious change remains uncertain. At the very least, however, they are highly suggestive, particularly in the way in which they link inner belief and outer events, the religious and the social.

An uncertainty about Douglas' theory concerns the exact nature of the social change which influences religious change. In brief, why were social conditions in the 1950s (when Ronald Knox wrote) so much more conducive to ritualistic, hierarchical, dogmatic religion than they were in 1970?

A standard all-purpose kind of answer immediately points to things like industrialization, technology, possibly atomic power as the explanation. The anti-ritualist makes a ritualistic reference to changed social conditions assumed to be explicable in such terms, and assumes also that everything relevant has been said. But this is intellectual laziness of the worst kind. To begin with, it is not self-evident that the effects of science and technology were somehow more powerful, or more disrupting, in the late 1960s than they had been in the early 1950s. Unrecognized as yet, America in 1970 was in fact poised on the edge of an industrial decline, which included certain kinds of technological decline, whereas not only America but the entire West was experiencing a massive industrial and technological recovery when Knox was writing and when the religious revival of the post-war period was at its peak. Furthermore, the correlation between technological development and religious dislocation is difficult to trace historically. Since about 1750 there have been recurring periods of intense technological innovation and also recurring periods of religious crisis, but it is not at all evident that they have had much to do with each other.

An alternative theory posits political and social upheaval as the crucial correlative to religious change or decline. There is greater empirical evidence for this, but not enough to be fully convincing. For example, two major social upheavals of the past fifty years —the Great Depression and World War II—had much deeper effects on society than virtually anything which happened during the 1960s and 1970s. Yet these upheavels did not undermine stable, traditional religion. If anything they seem to have strengthened it. The social disorders of the period after 1965 seem to lack, in the language of literary criticism, objective correlatives—there appears to have been no objective source of social dislocation proportionate to the discontent and disorientation which was manifest.

Two facts perhaps come closest to providing an adequate explanation. One is race. What did happen objectively, in the 1960s was a major change in the relationship of the races to one another in American society. A century-old pattern of segregation and subordination of black people was broken, a breakage which carried with it considerable trauma, conflict, and disorientation. However, in retrospect it is actually more impressive to note how little upheaval there was rather than how much. Except in the South, it was not so much a matter of upsetting deeply rooted and venerated patterns of living that had been sanctified by the custom of decades as it was of permitting yet a further degree of elasticity in a system that was habitually flexible and mobile already. Most white people proved to have no profound emotional stake in the institutions of segregation, and newer arrangements between the races did not seem to them like a cosmic reorientation of life. In addition, traditional Catholicism had been at least officially opposed to racial segregation for a long time. The maintenance of doctrinal and liturgical loyalties within the Church was hardly dependent on the maintenance of a segregated society.

A more convincing explanation has to do with the so-called "baby boom"—the phenomenon of an unprecedently large generation of young people born in the decades following World War II who, as they grew up, created a strain on the capacities of the social system at every key point, from kindergarten to prisons.[3] This explanation of social change does confront certain very obvious aspects of the phenomenon, including the fact that so much of social tension about 1965 was concentrated among the young, who collectively were the cutting edge of that change and discontent.

It has obvious relevance to religion as well, since it was also among the young that the key sources of religious discontent—with liturgy, with morality, with doctrine—were concentrated, and it was the young who seemed to have led the way out of the churches in large numbers. In every area of society it seemed to be at the point where traditional structures interacted with the new generation that the severest strains were felt.

However, it is also inadequate to accept this as a purely objective explanation, that is, as a social fact about which nothing could be done. What was ultimately significant about the youth culture of the 1960s was finally the fact that it was precisely a culture. It was not simply that over-crowded schools or unduly impersonal systems had alienated the young, although these were frequent explanations. It was rather that the huge generation of the young constituted a critical mass. They became acutely aware of their own size, their own strength, their own uniqueness, their own importance. Not only were they the largest generation to have been produced in American society, they were also the products of a uniquely child-centered society, of a system in which parents had lavished unprecedented material and spiritual attentions on their offspring. Children grew up persuaded that the resources of the world were rightly theirs, that there were no inherent limits on their expectations and aspirations.

The large "baby boom" was in part the result of prosperity—Americans after 1945 felt they could afford larger families. The mentality of the new generation was also in large measure a result of prosperity. Children who grow up in hard or precarious times imbibe from their parents a sense of limits, ways of restraining their own expectations. But the children of the post-1945 period imbibed exactly the opposite sense. Each year they experienced life as a little better, materially, than it had been the year before. This was a generation which took material satisfaction so much for granted that it could be anti-materialist and denounce its parents for money-grubbing. It was a generation which steadily expanded its expectations to the point where anything less than a perfect society (as the imagination conceived such a society) became intolerable. Closely joined to this cast of mind was a low level of personal toleration of frustration, and the two together largely account for the explosion of the youth culture of the 1960s.

Its causes, therefore, were less physical and social as such and more intellectual and moral. The youth culture merely crystallized certain attitudes which were widespread in the society, and it provided the means by which these attitudes could find respectable expression and social outlet. Thus it is misleading to think of the social upheaval of the 1960s as solely a youth phenomenon. Many older people welcomed the youth culture because it provided the rationale and the justification for their own "liberation" from traditional limits. In the Church, for example, radical changes sometimes took place at the behest of clergy who were ostensibly struggling to make religion relevant to the young but who in reality were experimenting with forms of religion which made they themselves feel more comfortable. The cultural revolution was in large measure a phenomenon of the older generation's imitating the practices of the youth culture.

Thus there was an at least semi-objective social revolution of sorts which took place in the 1960s—it was the relationship of the young to the old, of children to parents, of students to teachers which underwent radical change. This change was more profound, more-far-reaching, more disturbing to every aspect of society than the change in relationship between the races. It was the prelude to two equally radical changes of the next decade—the relationship between men and women, and the relationship of parents to children, in which parents with increasing boldness proclaimed that their own self-fulfillment took preference to whatever obligations they owed their offspring.

It was, not surprisingly, among the young of the 1960s that the sense of an infinite ego, of infinite possibilities for the self, was strongest. Such a sense has always been a characteristic of youth, greatly encouraged and expanded by the general cultural situation after 1945. The social revolution of the age was thus partially objective, in the sense that real social relationships did change, but it was an objective rela-

tionship based on subjective factors—the way people
thought and felt about reality. It was characteristic of
the mindset of the 1960s that even its revolutions had
to come about at its own willing and could not be
based on objective social factors.

The result, however, was still the kind of chaotic,
poorly defined, boundary-less society which Mary
Douglas sees as conducive to ritual breakdown. On
balance it would be hard to imagine a more confusing
reversal of social guideposts than one whereby the
relationship of the old and the young, of experience
and youth, of authority and tutelage, were reversed,
which is exactly what did happen. It was not merely
that youth challenged experience, student repudiated
teacher, child foreswore parent, it was the fact that, if
the claims made for the youth culture were taken seriously, it was necessary to reverse most of one's commonly held perceptions of reality. Youth not only had
to be given its freedom, it had to be acknowledged as
setting the tone and direction for the older generation
as well. The favored kind of manifesto of the late
1960s was that wherein an older person humbly acknowledged the errors of his or her own generation
and proudly admitted having adopted the values of
the young.

The implications of this for religion were immediate and obvious. For one thing, anything which
came through the vehicle of tradition suddenly
became suspect. For Catholicism this was a crucial

problem, since no religion has ever placed more emphasis on the importance of tradition. Suddenly,
however, creeds, liturgical practices, educational
materials, moral beliefs, and a whole range of other
things stood discredited, representative of modes of
belief which were now being systematically and sometimes savagely repudiated. What was from the past
was automatically suspect, salvageable only in rather
rare instances and by special indult.

Although the extent of this was not acknowledged
at the time, the new mindset in religion guaranteed
that nothing fixed and stable in religion could be re-
spected, because all such things were taken as representing the dead hand of the past pressing down on
the present. This included creeds, rituals, moral laws,
church hierarchies, virtually every aspect of church
life. Although the extent of the discontent was not at
first recognized, it became obvious before very long
that practically no aspect of historical Catholicism
could remain legitimate within the framework of the
emerging Counter-Culture.

The discrediting of traditional Catholicism took
place for two reasons. One was the fact that the notion of an infinitely free, infinitely expanding self was
completely incompatible with not just this or that
possibly "too rigid" aspect of church life but in the
end with any meaningful idea of dogma, moral law,
authoritative tradition, or hierarchical structure. The
other was the fact that, even where there was no

conscious animosity against that Catholicism, the confused social lines, as analyzed in Mary Douglas's theories, made such a religion incomprehensible to many. The traditional way in which creeds, catechisms, rituals, symbols—tradition itself—conveyed a sense of truth and continuity to people were now skewed.

The first manifestation of this, as with the larger Counter-Culture itself, was seemingly benign, or at least was experienced as such. Mary Douglas uses the term "effervescence" to describe the sense of relief, of liberation, of the release of pent-up energies which follows the collapse of social structure. The initial reaction is one of joyous freedom, of infinite possibility.

For a time religion had its principal meaning for many people simply in their systematic repudiation of whatever they had previously accepted as authoritative. The entire Catholic "renewal" movement was in a sense the progress, step by step, toward thinking and doing those things which had previously been inhibited, of failing to think and do those things which had been required. The "meaning" of this renewal was in the negation of meaning, although it took the participants a long time fully to realize this fact. For some the realization finally dawned that the ultimate liberation was from all religion, a logical consequence which they accepted. For others, however, religion came to be more and more a source of frustration and unhappiness, since the more they sought to "renew" the more they found it necessary to negate.

Along with this went the dream of a wholly spontaneous spiritual rebirth, a religious counterpart of the secular utopianism which characterized both the New Left and Counter-Culture. For a time everything which could be represented as truly "creative," "free," spontaneous—in liturgy especially—gained automatic authority.

But as Douglas points out, as the effervescence settles down, the results of this kind of ritual freedom is confusion, alienation, disorientation. The new, spontaneous, unfixed modes of worship are simply too weak to express profoundly held truths. The soul wanders lost, uncertain of its relationship either to God or to its own community. The disorder of the community in part dictates the disorder of worship, but the latter in turn also contributes to the further unravelling of community bonds. As Douglas says, all self-proclaimed "renewal" movements are anti-ritualist, promising as they do a spontaneous source of recovery. They also tend to be millenarian—the religion no longer possesses the power to understand and validate present social existence and thus looks forward to the end of time and the final obliteration of all structures. In Catholicism, in keeping with her theory of the importance of bodily imagery, Douglas postulates that first the Incarnation becomes unimaginable, then Christ's bodily presence in the Eucharist.

In short, the central mysteries of the Catholic faith are lost. (Although these quite sensitive points were often studiously avoided in the 1970s, it became increasingly evident that for many partisans of Catholic renewal Christ was regarded as a great human being, only problematically as God, and that the Eucharist was primarily a symbol of community.)

Thus the feature which all religious movements of the 1970s had in common was their expressiveness —whatever else they did, they promised a religion which welled out of the effervescent experiences of the devotee, was founded four-square on that experience. This was true of both Christian and non-Christian forms of religiosity, of both new creations and of the revival of older forms like pentecostalism.

Again both the "optimistic" and the "pessimistic" currents of the age tended towards the same result. The former encouraged people to think that within themselves they had all the spiritual resources necessary to find whatever truth was worth knowing. A kind of self-divinization occurred, in which it was considered quite legitimate to equate one's own self-stirrings with the actions of God. One's own conscience was practically deified. From the pessimistic side, many people simply found themselves bereft of all spiritual resources outside themselves. They might have welcomed the aid of tradition, creed, hierarchy, genuine authority, but often they were unaware that such things even existed, or else the culture had rendered these things so weak and pallid that they were of no use.

From both sides, therefore, personal experience was for many people the only certain spiritual reality. Like those caught in some great historical cataclysm, they had to reinvent the spiritual wheel, and keep doing so. In the solipsistic world which the Counter-Culture had made, only powerful emotions were real, and their reality was guaranteed only by their increasing power, as with drug doses. The imagination was so enfeebled that it could not comprehend the reality of anything outside the ken of its own direct and necessarily limited experience. Thus what religion there was was likely to be passionate and emotional but also shallow and almost always narrow. Often it was unclear whether the religious believer was truly worshipping God, or merely his own experience.

Chapter 5

Gnosticism

AS mentioned in Chapter One, perhaps the most sig-nigificant development in the history of Ronald Knox's chosen subject has been the discovery, since he wrote, of a cache of documents representing the actual writings of the early Christian Gnostics. A sub-ject to which Knox paid only glancing attention would have to loom very large in any modern rewrit-ing of his book.

Gnosticism was a movement in ancient religion and philosophy[1] which predated Christianity. It had its pagan, Jewish, and Christian forms, and, altogether, it was one of the most powerful and pervasive intel-lectual and religious movements of the late antique world, its influence difficult to overestimate. At the same time, since it was ultimately defeated, it has been largely lost from historical memory, known principally to specialized scholars, its one-time influ-ence greatly underestimated.

Fundamentally, Gnosticism was a kind of dualism,

that is, it posited the division of the universe into two radically distinct and opposed realms, roughly those of light and darkness or of spirit and flesh, each presided over by its own divinity. These divinities are coequal with one another, engaged in a never-ending war which will lead to no final victory for either side but will lead gradually to the final sorting out of the two kingdoms.

Human nature finds itself thus in a precarious middle state, divided between the two respective kingdoms, lost, alienated, even imprisoned. The principal task of human existence is to extricate the true self from this alien prison. Here the name of the movement becomes significant. It derives from the Greek word *"gnosis"* or "knowledge," and it refers to a special, esoteric knowledge which the individual must possess in order to become free of the prison of worldly existence.

The esoteric nature of that knowledge is crucial, because it automatically divides the world between the masses who are ignorant or who suffer from illusion and a small elite who alone possess the truth. Whereas Christianity preached exoteric truth, that is, a gospel available to anyone who would listen and obey, Gnosticism held that genuine religious teachings, including those of Christ, are hidden and secret and can only be understood by those who possess the key which Gnostic initiation and Gnostic discipline alone provide.

Perhaps the most important point of conflict between orthodox Christianity and Christian Gnosticism was precisely over the nature of the universe. Orthodox Christianity frankly acknowledged that it was an offshoot of Judaism. Thus the Jewish Scriptures were part of the basic deposit of faith of Christianity itself. Central to this was the belief that God the Father, to whom Christ made constant reference in his public teaching, was the Yahweh of the Jews, the creator of the universe. To the Gnostics, however, the universe was an evil place, the domain of the god of darkness. Hence the good Father to whom Jesus referred could not be the creator god of the Old Testament.

An important practical aspect of Gnosticism was its strong sense of the meaninglessness of existence as understood in ordinary terms. All the established keys to understanding truth—reason, moral law, public order, etc.—were regarded as illusory or worse. Man in nature was trapped and could only escape through the acquisition of the secret key. Hans Jonas has pointed out that, with its equivalent emphasis on the "absurdity" of existence, ancient Gnosticism bore a notable resemblance to modern Existentialism.

Although the existence of Christian versions of Gnosticism was known ever since ancient times, the full importance of this movement only came to light with the discovery of some ancient manuscripts in Egypt just after world War II. For years the editing and publication of these were delayed, but they finally came to public light in the late 1970s. The most influential study of their significance is a semi-popular book by Elaine Pagels.[2]

Pagels is also extremely interested in the contemporary relevance of Gnosticism and, in essence, her presentation of the subject focuses mainly on the significant points of conflict between orthodoxy and Gnosticism, with reference to the recurrence of those same conflicts in modern times. Although she herself seems primarily sympathetic to Gnosticism, her argument can also be used to support orthodoxy.

In particular, what Pagels has shown, possibly not altogether wittingly, is that much of what passes for the religion of "renewal" in the contemporary world has much more in common with historic Gnosticism than with orthodoxy. Her book makes it harder for radical innovators to claim continuity with the historic Church, and makes it more obvious that they are trying to reopen questions which were resolved when Christianity was still quite young (for the most part during the second century).

Perhaps the key point which underlies all the others is the Gnostic preference for symbolic rather than literal understandings of religious teaching. Some Gnostics, for example, held that Jesus was not really crucified, and there was wide agreement among them that the Resurrection was to be understood as a symbolic, spiritual appearance. Those Christians who held that Christ had risen bodily were ridiculed by the Gnostics. Those who believed such a thing were considered, naive, carnal-minded, lacking in sophistication and deeper understanding. Whether or not Christ physically appeared to his disciples a few days following his death was considered unimportant. What was important was that the believer encounter the risen Christ spiritually in the present.

Similarly the Gnostics ridiculed a concern for doctrinal orthodoxy. Whereas the Catholics increasingly insisted that correct belief depended on a careful and faithful preservation of apostolic teaching, fidelity to tradition, the Gnostics were much more inclined to emphasize "creativity" with respect to doctrine. The believer was expected to internalize received teaching, ponder it, meditate on it, and pass it on transformed. The discovery of new and previously hidden meanings was considered far more important than simple fidelity to tradition. Indeed, from the Gnostic viewpoint, such fidelity was precisely the kind of superficial understanding of the Gospel which prevented the majority from attaining the hidden key to genuine and liberating truth.

The major thesis of Pagels' work is that the doctrinal conflict between the orthodox and the Gnostics reflected a conflict over church structure and government. Emphasis on doctrinal orthodoxy in turn implied a structure of authority which could determine the content of that orthodoxy. Conversely, in a community which emphasized individuality of doctrinal interpretation, such authority was not only unnecessary, it would even be a hindrance to the genuine discovery of truth. She believes the orthodox placed so much emphasis on the literal historical character of Christ's Resurrection because authority in the Church therefore rested with those who had seen the risen Christ (especially Peter) and their successors (apostolic succession).

The importance of the episcopacy had been already emphasized in the early second century by Clement of Rome and Ignatius of Antioch. In Pagels' view it was no accident that some of the strongest opponents of the Gnostics, notably Irenaeus of Lyons, were bishops. What was at stake in the Gnostic controversy was, among other things, the validity of the hierarchical church organized around a monarchical bishop.

The Gnostics tended to produce structureless groups, all members roughly equal, with no designated hierarchy. Critics like Irenaeus regarded these as self-evidently false and contrary to the divine law. But to the Gnostics they were the natural outcome of their particular conception of truth.

An important and obviously timely feature of Gnosticism was what might, without exaggeration, be called its feminist tendencies. Some Gnostic writings contained references to God the Mother, for example, and Gnostic communities, having foresworn hierarchy, seem to have regarded men and women as equals in contrast to the Catholic mainstream which permitted the priesthood and the episcopacy only to males. Irenaeus commented that women seemed to be attracted to heresy in disproportionate numbers.

Pagels believes there was a kind of feminist revolution going on in late antiquity, which orthodox Catholicism successfully resisted.

Not surprisingly, the Gnostics placed little emphasis on the externals of religion. Their difference, even contempt, toward orthodoxy of doctrine has already been noted. In addition, they placed little emphasis on the sacraments, except in a highly symbolic, spiritualized way. Too great a reliance on the sacraments they regarded as superstitious, evidence of a magical view of life.

Perhaps most surprising about the early Gnostics was the fact that, apparently, they deemphasized the importance of martyrdom, which mainstream Christians regarded as the ultimate seal of faith. Gnostics did not condemn martyrdom altogether, but they justified their followers in evading it and gave it relatively little positive value. In essence, this attitude seems to have derived once again from their deemphasis on external events and too "literal" an understanding of Christian doctrine. Conflict to the death with paganism was unnecessary if Christian doctrine could be understood in various ways.

Obviously the elaborate cosmic and metaphysical theories of Gnosticism are held by very few Christians today. Such theories are, in fact, very remote from contemporary Christian sensibility. However, in certain respects Gnosticism has a very modern look about it.

Even with regard to its theories about the cosmos,

it should be noted that the cultural atmosphere of the 1970s, what has been called here a religious tropical jungle, had a lot in common with historical Gnosticism. The preoccupation with finding a hidden key to the universe, belief in magic, the sense of alienation requiring an esoteric form of knowledge to escape— all manifested themselves in some of the various non-Christian religious movements of the 1970s. On one level orthodox Christianity was contemptuously dismissed by many people for precisely similar reasons for which it was dismissed in its early centuries.

Within Christianity itself, certain resemblances to historical Gnosticism are striking, even though divorced from Gnosticism's cosmic and philosophical roots.

One of the most obvious is the rejection of "literal-minded" understandings of Christian doctrine. Historical Catholicism has set great store by doctrinal orthodoxy, meaning a firm and unambiguous adherence to verbal formulations of doctrine. Probably no aspect of historical Catholicism has come under more relentless attack than that. At every turn specters of the Inquisition have been raised. Above all, contemporary Catholics have emphasized, over and over again, the ambiguities and inadequacies of all doctrinal statements, the ways in which such statements are open to a variety of interpretations. Like the Gnostics, they have valued imaginative reinterpretation of historical credal statements much more than fidelity to apostolic teaching. Emphasis on traditional orthodoxy has been taken as evidence of a narrow, rigid, uncreative mindset.

As with the historical Gnostics, this interest in the innovative and symbolic uses of doctrine has concentrated especially on key doctrines like the Resurrection. One of the best contemporary dividing lines in theology is precisely the treatment of the Resurrection, between those who insist on the empty tomb of Easter morning and Christ's bodily rising from the dead and those who denigrate the literal-mindedness of this approach and insist that the mystery of the Resurrection is elusive and ultimately spiritual. Its importance for the individual believer is deemed much greater than what may have happened on the first Easter morning. The "encounter" with the risen Christ in one's own life (however that may be understood) is considered far more significant than whether the New Testament accounts of the Resurrection are historically accurate.

As with historical Gnosticism, this emphasis on the primarily symbolic significance of doctrine also tends to blend with an indifference and even hostility toward an organized, structured, hierarchical church. For one thing, as Pagels suggests, such a church has historically been connected with the necessity of correct doctrine. Thus, those who desire the maximum freedom of improvisation in matters of doctrine will be restive under the discipline of a highly structured church. Besides this, however, a free-wheeling and largely symbolic approach to doctrine makes it impossible to justify any fixed ecclesiastical structure. All such structures are inevitably seen as historical accretions, at best responsive to the needs of a particular age. In general the less formal the structure the better.

In addition, the spirit of the age also favors a minimally structured church. This is not only because of the dominance of democracy as the favored form of government in the modern West, it is also because of the cultural mood which borders on anarchy, the progressive deterioration and destruction of all social structure, as discussed in Chapter Four. Objective structure is inevitably experienced as an imposition on the self, which must somehow be negated. Episcopacy is particularly the point of this conflict, and the "good" bishop is the man who functions like a kindly and indulgent uncle but never seeks to exercise the authority inherent in his office.

The feminist aspect of Gnosticism is of course obvious. If Pagels' theories are correct, historical Catholicism faced the question of women's role in the Church quite early in its existence and made its rejection of "women's liberation" part of its self-identity. Thus, the feminist movement within the Church seeks not merely a natural development from earlier doctrine and practice but a negation of the same. It seeks to reopen questions that were closed eighteen centuries ago. It seeks a church which would bear little resemblance to the one which has been known for all those intervening centuries. It would, in short, be a church which was scarcely Catholic at all, as Catholic has been understood historically.

It is important to recognize that there are prior questions beyond feminism itself, which are often not discussed. The issue is not merely whether women may or may not be priests. It is also a question of how such decisions are made in the Church. The advocates of women's ordination commonly argue from the "why not?" perspective. Implicitly their syllogism runs, "Women want to be priests. Women can be priests. Therefore, women should be priests." Added to this is the notion that it is cruel and "uncompassionate" not to allow women to be ordained. In other words, ordination is treated as though it were essentially a function of desire. It fits very well with the Gnostic attitude which permits the individual to manipulate Christian doctrines "creatively." Is God Mother? The Scriptures do not say so, but if certain devotees "need" a feminist god they should have one.

Contemporary feminism is part of the general process of seeking to obliterate all social structure. Again prescinding from the specific question of whether women should be priests, feminism insists with dogmatic rigor that all social distinctions based on gender must be denied. The coherence and plausibility of historical Catholicism are further destroyed as the relationship between the sexes is radically redefined. The male priesthood, a notable feature of that Catholicism, comes to seem merely a form of illegitimate oppression. The very identity of God becomes confused

and problematical. Much of the worship of the
Church, and even much of the Scripture, is dismissed
as infected with "sexism." It might also be suggested
that Catholic feminism gains much of its present intensity from a previous social dislocation—many of
the "reforms" in convent life made the identity of being a nun no longer plausible and reduced convent life
to chaos. Thus, nuns in large numbers reached out to
the possibility of becoming priests.

The contemporary Church is also in certain important ways anti-sacramental. The diatribes of some
contemporary liturgists against "magical" understandings of the sacraments, against all ritual, would
have fit in quite well with Gnostic polemics of the second century. The truth is that many contemporary
partisans of "renewal" in the Church find the sacraments an embarrassment, and for the same reasons
the Gnostics did—the sacraments are too physical,
too seemingly arbitrary and fixed, too external. True
religious meaning is, for such people, interior only,
all symbolic manifestations troublesome. This is especially obvious with regard to the Eucharist where, if
the doctrine of the Real Presence has not been formally denied, it has nonetheless been "explained" to
such an extent that for many people it effectively no
longer exists. Other sacraments have been also appropriately downgraded. There is obsessive fear lest Baptism be taken as a magical rite. Confession has been
abandoned by large numbers of people, often with
clerical encouragement. Marital vows are no longer

taken as sacred, nor as a sign that God gives sufficient grace to those who have entered into Matrimony. Much energy is rather expended proving that apparent sacramental marriages are not actually valid. Confirmation is a problematical and uncertain rite which some would suppress. The binding nature of Holy Orders is negated in much the same way Matrimony is, and the Last Anointing has been redefined to rob it of much of its significance.

Wholly unconscious, there is, in fact, a kind of remnant of the Gnostic view of cosmic alienation here. Contemporary avant-garde Catholics have little trouble understanding sacraments as celebrations of human community; this is their favored notion of the Eucharist, for example, with the handshake of peace the high point of the service. What they are incapable of doing is imagining these carnal rituals as genuine epiphanies of the divine, as transcendently meaningful acts. The universe is for these people cold and silent, the only warm sound the echo of human voices.

Contemporary avant-garde Christians do not, any more than did the Gnostics, reject martyrdom outright. But like the Gnostics they do deemphasize it. Today's Christians are likely to find martyrdom something of a historical embarrassment. The martyrs appear in retrospect as distressingly literal-minded and fanataical. Their conflicts with the pagan authorities could, it seems, often have been avoided with a little more show of reason. Martyrs of the Reformation period, like those of England and Wales, seem to have been quite un-ecumenical. Contemporary Christians are likely to find martyrdom incomprehensible except as it fits into familiar political categories. Thus, for example, the radical Jesuit activist Daniel Berrigan says he would not die for the Eucharist except insofar as it had an "extraordinarily secularized" kind of meaning.[3]

Unlike the historical Gnostics, today's avant-garde Catholics do not profess literally esoteric wisdom, that is, hidden and secret knowledge accessible only to a few. In practice, however, they often do profess an elitism rather similar to the Gnostics' own. They have little trouble, with the Gnostics, in positing a pure and truly Christian elite at odds with a largely ignorant and corrupt church, a corruption which extends to the highest authorities of that church. Although the new elite does not profess to have esoteric knowledge, they do indeed posit for themselves a superior understanding of religion, an understanding which renders obsolete the old-fashioned beliefs and practices of others, including many bishops and even the Pope. The Gnostics of the second century offered the key to wisdom in the form of arcane knowledge gradually imparted to initiates. Today's neo-Gnostic, if the term can be used, believes such knowledge is accessible if one reads certain books by certain authors, attends certain seminars, etc. At each point the "expert" is said to have a deeper and more comprehensive understanding of Christian truth than others, including the ostensible guardians of that truth, the bishops. A sign of religious enlightenment is that one often holds doctrinal positions which are almost the reverse of those commonly held, and those whose understanding of their faith is not appropriately up-to-date are continually excoriated for that fact. (Thus certain theologians continually remind Catholics that the bishops received their theological training twenty or more years ago and it is now obsolete.)

The Gnostic element in this also manifests itself in the sense which so many of the avant-garde have that a "true" understanding of Christianity will be shocking to the sensibilities of the many, will in fact often be the reverse of what has been commonly believed. Much energy has been expended inculcating an understanding of sacraments, the nature of the Church, morality, etc., which is virtually contradictory of what has been thought of as genuine Catholicism. There has been talk to the effect that only about the time of the Second Vatican Council has the "real" meaning of Catholicism come to light, certainly a very Gnostic kind of idea, and that this "real" meaning has been hidden from the masses and even from the official church leadership.

Although Pagels does not emphasize the fact, Gnosticism seems, in essence, to have been the rejection of the historical nature of Christianity, something which it also has in common with some contemporary Catholicism. For the Gnostics, embarrassment over Christ's actual bodily resurrection, for example, and their uncontrollable tendency to reduce every Christian doctrine to symbolism or allegory, stems from the determination that no aspect of Christian teaching should be tied down to any concrete and specific historical event. For the Gnostics, the Incarnation is at best a problematical doctrine, since in Gnostic cosmology it is almost impossible to understand how a good God could have taken flesh. Thus the Gnostic emphasis on symbolism aims to elevate all Christian belief above history, to make it independent of any concrete and limiting circumstances.

In principle, contemporary revisionist Catholics believe in the Incarnation and do not denigrate the world of matter. However, they suffer from the same Gnostic failure of imagination—inability to conceive that divine transcendence could truly be mediated to man through the realm of history. Thus, much contemporary Christology, for example, is taken up with explaining away the Incarnation in the full sense— Jesus is presented as essentially a man, in whom God may have been "present" in a special way.

In particular, however, it is the historicity of the Church which is a profound embarrassment to the contemporary Gnostics. They cannot comprehend that Christ should have founded such an institution, that it should have taken the form that it did, that it should have survived so many centuries. For them it is mired in matter and particularity. Its history especially is embarrassing. They prefer a church which is essentially an invisible community, the form of which can be endlessly altered in keeping with the needs of the imagination.

It is finally here that the key to understanding Gnosticism can perhaps be found. The movement flourished in late antiquity, at a time when the settled contours of the world—political, social, religious, philosophical—were being radically altered. All historians agree that, whatever else it was, Gnosticism was a response to the anxiety and rootlessness which this situation generated. In Mary Douglas' terms, Gnosticism can be seen as the effervescence of a society which was disintegrating.

The key to Gnosticism, therefore, is the primacy it gives to human desire, human preference, human will and imagination. It denigrates the world, makes it less than real, so that the world can become essentially an emanation of the self. In terms already used here, this had its "optimistic" and its "pessimistic" aspects, which converged—Gnosticism taught people simultaneously to despair over the universe and to imagine infinite possibilities open to them in the universe of the imagination instead.

Gnosticism promised knowledge or enlightenment to its followers, and Pagels translates one of its key terms as "fulfillment." One of its major differences with orthodox Christianity was its rejection of, or at least radical deemphasis of, the notion of sin. The Gnostics preferred to think of humanity as suffering from ignorance, a condition which was in principle correctable, rather than sin, a condition built into human nature and not susceptible to healing by human action alone. What man needs, according to Gnostic doctrine, is enlightenment, not salvation.

The contemporary relevance of all this is too obvious to require belaboring. Today's avant-garde Christians are similarly uncomfortable with the notion of sin, and for similar reasons. They, too, want to preserve a view of man which is in principle perfectible, which is not hampered by any inherent moral flaws.

Pagels notices parallels between Gnosticism and certain kinds of present-day psychotherapy. For example, the Gnostics taught that self-knowledge is tantamount to knowledge of God, and in the extreme they also taught that God and self are one. Gnosticism was in reality a form of self-deification. Not only did it reject the "narrow" understanding of events like the Resurrection, and the "narrow" understanding of the Church, but also an equally "narrow," because objective, notion of God. For the Gnostics God, too, had to be a creation of the human imagination. The self expanded gradually until, in effect, it became God. Pagels observes that, unlike the orthodox Christian idea that man is saved by the gratuitous act of God, Gnosticism taught that the key to salvation lies in the self, an idea dear to many contemporary kinds of psychotherapy.

Hans Jonas emphasizes an aspect of ancient Gnosticism which Pagels generally ignores—its antinomianism. Jonas in fact goes so far as to speak of the Gnostics as "moral nihilists" and as "libertines."

This is paradoxical because, in theory, Gnosticism taught a rigorous and puritanical ethic, because of its official doctrine denigrating the world of matter. But throughout the history of religion this paradox recurs —a religion which condemns the flesh ends by tolerating a chaotic sexual ethic, precisely because it can perceive no positive meaning in it. If marriage, for example, has no sacramental significance, then it is hardly any different from concubinage. There are hints of a similarity here with certain contemporary kinds of Christianity in which, as marriage is more and more downgraded, vigorous attempts are made to give equal moral status to homosexuality or unmarried cohabitation.

Jonas, however, stresses the intellectual relativism of the Gnostics. For them the universe had no intelligible intellectual structure. Thus the ancient emphasis on natural law could have no meaning. Gnostics made a point of expressing skepticism about all commonly held moral beliefs. Over and over again they emphasized that law cannot be absolute, and under Gnostic influence the concept of law grew weaker and weaker.

On one level this situation sometimes justified even moral promiscuity, for if Gnosticism did not exactly condone such behavior, it undermined the means whereby that behavior could be subjected to meaningful criticism. It also tended to regard excessive veneration for the law as worse.

Gnostic libertinism was also an emanation from the sense of the sovereign, infinite self previously discussed. Just as the Gnostics would not invest particular actions with transcendent positive significance, so they could not condemn any action in absolute terms. All human actions were seen as subject to the sovereign will, and Jonas notes that for the Gnostics, as the modern Existentialists, values were a projection of that will. The Gnostic concept of human freedom demanded that all actions be at least theoretically open to human choice. The parallels with certain kinds of contemporary Christianity are too obvious to need belaboring.

Gnosticism is not a religious movement which has enjoyed an unbroken underground existence since ancient times. However, it appears to be a religious attitude which is a natural one at certain historical periods. Ronald Knox treated it as a minor footnote to history. Its central importance can now be recognized.

Chapter 6

Political Gnosticism

AT first, political Christianity, or a Christianity pre-occupied with social justice, may seem far removed from the kind of religious enthusiasm here discussed. The former is objective, oriented around palpable social conditions; the latter tends to be subjective and egocentric. The former frequently falls under the suspicion of being a merely secularized religion; the latter can almost be defined as an excess of religion.

However, a deeper look shows aspects of political Christianity which definitely fall within the framework of enthusiasm here developed. A major thesis of this book is that the cultural and religious references have changed so radically since Ronald Knox's day that enthusiasm now sometimes expresses itself in ways that would have been unrecognizable to him, and in ways which are sometimes also quite secular.

The political philosopher Eric Voeglin has discussed Gnosticism as a perennial Christian heresy. Extending it beyond the period of the early centuries when it was overtly such, he sees it as a recurring temptation of Christianity, often presenting itself as orthodox, sometimes not recognizably Christian at all but nonetheless having deep Christian roots. The source of this heresy, according to Voeglin, is the fact that Christian faith is a "heroic adventure of soul" which is both .difficult and subtle. There is, consequently, recurring pressure on Christians to desist from the demanding adventure and to accept counterfeits of faith which are in some sense easier, if not in terms of physical demands then in terms of the spiritual striving required. The most seductive of these is the "creation of a terrestrial paradise."[1]

At every step in the analysis of enthusiasm it is necessary to recall that its principal traits are all distortions of genuine and essential aspects of Christianity. Heresy is, in essence, a cancer, cells in the body which expand uncontrollably to threaten the life of the whole. In proportion, those cells are essential to the body's well being. So it is with social justice. There have been times in the Church's history when social justice has been neglected, even in fact denied. The post-conciliar period has tended rather to see a concept of social justice which is distorted in two ways —by making it so absolute that all other aspects of Christianity are, in effect, forced to prove their right to exist (as in the frequently expressed fear that prayer will "distract" people from social concerns), and in a concept of social justice which is absolutist and utopian, which, in effect, equates justice and charity with certain quasi-totalitarian political experiments.

The development of this distorted social sense was, in part, an outgrowth of the Second Vatican Council's emphasis on such concerns, an emphasis which was hardly new (there was a lively tradition of it dating back at least to *Rerum Novarum* in 1891) but which was apparently new to some people. This accounts for the measurable impetus it received about 1965, strongly abetted in America by the civil-rights movement and later the anti-war movement. However, the fierce dedication and virtual absolutism with which it was embraced by so many, especially by priests and nuns, was also a result of the collapse of so much traditional spirituality and traditional forms of religious life. People who had committed themselves to a life which demanded the totality of their selves were sometimes left bereft by "renewal" programs which had made that life shapeless and emptied of all meaning. They frequently found new meaning in various political crusades.

The interest in social causes is not itself an indication of religious aberrancy, since such a concern has always been, to one degree or another, a mark of authentic Christianity. Nor is the intensity of the concern necessarily evidence of unbalance—truly holy people are able to be equally intense about everything they do. Rather the distortion of social justice among Christians resides in the cultic character it often takes on, the nearly totalitarian utopianism with which it is invested.

A surprising number of Ronald Knox's characteristics of enthusiasm are applicable to contemporary movements for social justice, once adjustment is made for changed conditions over thirty years:

Excessive piety. Obviously this is not true of piety in the conventional sense. Many Christian advocates of social justice seem almost secular in their outlook, and most probably have little use for piety as traditionally understood. However, in terms of Knox's understanding of it as a claim to superior holiness, a kind of pharasaical self-righteousness, it does apply. Many Christians who would confess wide-ranging uncertainty over most theological and moral issues are absolutely convinced of the rightness of their stand on contemporary political and economic questions.

Schism. Movements for social change have often been characterized by splits and divisions, because their members hold to their beliefs with such intensity that they are reluctant to compromise, quick to suspect betrayal. In this there is an almost exact parallel with sectarian religious movements. Socialism in its widest sense, for example, has been characterized by numerous such divisions over the years. There have been some similar developments in the Christian Left. However, more important has been the tendency of at least certain elements of the Catholic Left to exist in a state of virtual schism from the main body of the Church. They have a strong sense of the righteousness of their own position and are angered by the failure of the rest of the Church to share it, or at least to share it with much real commitment. Despite some efforts to build bridges to the main body of the Church, many Catholic leftists exist in a religious world largely of their own creation, alienated from the majority of the people in the pew and from the majority of the hierarchy as well.

Charismatic authority. Like the religious enthusiasts who have little use for church office and concede authority to the person who seems to possess spiritual gifts, many Catholic leftists concede authoritative leadership only to those from their own ranks who seem to possess the proper qualities of political concern and passion. They speak frequently and easily of "prophecy," and in terms of the familiar Old Testament tension between priest and prophet they come down unhesitatingly in favor of the prophet. Prophecy is understood, however, as public espousal of properly radical political opinions. When an occasional hierarchical figure appears to be a prophet in this sense, he is welcomed, especially since this tends to place the weight of the Church itself behind radical ideas. However, the coincidence of hierarchy and prophecy is regarded as merely fortuitous. Ordinarily it is expected that the established leadership of the Church is not prophetic, or is insufficiently so. Real religious leadership must therefore be looked for elsewhere. Contemporary Catholic radicals often seem convinced that the Spirit breathes on them directly, inspiring and validating their political stands.

Ultrasupernaturalism. Obviously most of the Catholic Left does not manifest this trait in the way in which Knox assigned it to his enthusiasts. However, as noted, the Catholic Left often seems to claim a kind of direct divine inspiration with regard to contemporary social issues. Where others might profess uncertainty over the complexity of practical problems, the Left usually knows precisely what God's will is in a given case, e.g., American policy toward South Africa or the construction of nuclear power plants. Sometimes a generally accepted position of the Left seems to go against the bulk of Catholic tradition, e.g., with regard to capital punishment. In those cases a kind of direct, contemporary divine inspiration is, in effect, claimed.

Global pessimism. Here the evidence seems ambivalent. Often Catholic leftists seem to be Pelagians —they do not really believe in original sin and they seem to believe that social reforms will bring an end to evil in the world. However, in practice, they also tend to be extremely pessimistic about most existing social orders, and especially those of the West, where the majority of Christian leftists live. It is impossible to read their statements without coming away with the impression that to live in America is to participate in an almost hopelessly corrupt society, with redemption assigned to a saving remnant.

Anti-intellectualism. This is not a universal characteristic of the Catholic Left, which has produced some fairly sophisticated social thinkers. However, it tends to be true of the movement at the practical level. For example, Daniel Berrigan rather frequently sneers at his Jesuit brothers engaged in "safe" academic and scholarly careers.[2] The Catholic Left has in large measure been formed by the political attitudes of the 1960s. Among those attitudes is impatience with anything which does not seem to yield immediate results. The world must be changed now, and leisured thought is often regarded as a betrayal of that urgent task. Some Catholic radicals treat all speculative theology in this way, and Church leaders are often criticized because they concern themselves with "useless" questions like the divinity of Christ instead of merely plunging into the social struggle.

Theocracy. Catholic leftists would not establish a literal theocracy, that is, rule by the church or by religious officials. However, having identified the pressing moral issues of the age, they do seem inclined to establish the rule of the virtuous. There is often an impatience with the established political process, in which morally insensitive people have a majority voice, and a preference for direct action by which the virtuous can determine the outcome of public policy. On the whole, however, Catholic radicals seem more comfortable on the outside of power, even though they may dream of a society in which the virtuous rule.

Millenarianism. This is perhaps the most important way in which the Catholic Left shares the outlook of Knox's religious enthusiasts. For the most part this is, again, not in a literal sense. Few Catholic radicals probably believe that the end of the world is at hand, or the last days. Many may not believe that the world will have an end in the traditional Christian sense.

However, they do tend to think of themselves as living in a crucial era of history, in which great and profoundly transforming movements are underway. Often lacking historical perspective, they do not realize how often in the past these same expectations have arisen and have severely disappointed those who held them. The Christian Left's perspective is at least vaguely Marxist, and Marxism in particular has been promising its adherents the final definitive revolution for well over a century, each time producing only disillusionment.

Voeglin's "terrestial paradise" is the form which contemporary Catholic millenarianism tends to take —not a prediction of the end of the world or the reign of the saints in the traditional sense but the emergence of the perfectly just society. This expectation is for more than simply a steady improvement in the level of justice in the world. Since religious meaning has been invested in the realization of the just society, it is necessary to foresee the emergence of a society which has abolished all injustice, which marks the realization of the Christian ideal in this world.

Certain contemporary movements are therefore conceded enormous historical significance, as movements which have grasped the key to millenia of injustice and will, if they are only permitted, bring injustice to an end. The movements of "revolution" in the "Third World" are the chief objects of that expectation. Certain domestic movements like feminism are conceded similar importance.

Such expectations have a tendency to end in support of totalitarian regimes, so long as those regimes are "progressive" in character and employ Marxist rhetoric about oppression and liberation. (Both Cuba and China have been favored in recent years.) This sympathy for leftist totalitarianism is not always total. Sometimes it stops at merely making excuses for leftist abuses, short of complete support. However, it is also not accidental. The Catholic radical is drawn to totalitarian regimes in part precisely because they are totalitarian—it requires such a regime to get beyond democratic gradualism. Only such a regime can justify the total gift of self which the religious radical desires to make.[3]

Mysticism. There seems to be little real interest in mysticism among Catholic leftists. However, there are those who seek to redefine mysticism in such a way as to make it serviceable to leftist causes.[4]

Antinomianism. Many Catholic leftists are literal antinomians in that they engage in and justify acts of disobedience against a civil law which is deemed unjust. There have been numerous such actions with respect to racial justice, war, nuclear energy, and other issues. (There have also been some engaged in by a different set of people, in protest of abortion.)

Acts of civil disobedience can in principle be justified in Christian morality because Christians are obviously bound by the higher law, the law of God, rather than an unjust human law. The real question is the authority of the moral law itself.

There is a certain element of what can be called moral conservatism in the Catholic Left, especially with regard to the sensitive acts having to do with sexuality. Some Catholic leftists show little disposition to revise traditional moral teachings, although they frequently indicate that these are overemphasized.

There is, however, another element of the Catholic Left which does take an attitude of some casualness to the traditional moral law. Any direct familiarity with the movement in the 1960s, for example, revealed that casual or irregular sex, drug use, and other signs of the hedonistic society were not unknown there. Numerous religious who got involved in radical causes abandoned their vows of chastity and left the religious life. When Philip Berrigan revealed his marriage to a nun, Elizabeth McAllister, he seemed to proclaim defiantly a right to repudiate that vow, imposed by a repressive Church.[5] Some Catholic radicals went through the same arc of development described in Chapter 3 with respect to the secular culture.

Lust for Martyrdom. Desire for martyrdom and obedient acceptance of it when it comes are often difficult to distinguish without intimate knowledge of the martyr. It can merely be pointed out that the Catholic Left has made martrydom or quasi-martyrdom (prison sentences) a major mark of its existence, one of the things which has most sharply defined it and in which it has taken pride. The movement has spoken repeatedly about "witness," for which "martyr" is the Greek word. Acts of deliberate civil disobedience are almost inevitably likely to result in arrest and imprisonment, and the Catholic Left has attached supreme importance to precisely such acts.

Invisible Church. As already noted, the Catholic Left has a tendency to disregard the main body of the Church in favor of its own gathered groups. It shows little interest in and respect for the "institutional Church," which is regarded as deeply implicated in the sinfulness of the society as a whole. Although this belief is not always articulated, it does have a sense of the primary Christian community as composed of like-minded souls from all denominations, who have escaped the compromising corruption of their respective denominations. These have spiritual unity with one another even if there is little formal unity, because the latter is not ultimately important. Sometimes membership in this invisible church is based exclusively on commitment to social causes, not on religious belief. Thus the Berrigan circle could give communion to a secularized Moslem, explaining that the Eucharist was not to be understood in a narrow way.[6]

Desire for results. As previously indicated, this is a common characteristic of the Catholic Left, related to its sometime anti-intellectualism. If some elements of the movement can be regarded as connoiseurs of lost causes (as have many leftists and rightists over the years), most do manifest a strong desire to see tangible and far-reaching social changes within their lifetimes. They are impatient with all formulas for long-range change, suspicious of gradualism.

Experimentalism. In common with many self-consciously avant-garde Catholics, the Catholic Left tends to rely on experience—personal and social—as its primary guide in religion. Often, therefore, its ideas seem less a derivation from a Catholic understanding of society than a use of convenient ideas from Catholic social thought to bolster positions arrived at in other ways. There is no particular element of ecstatic experience in this social Catholicism, but there is much emphasis on powerful and transforming personal experiences of oppression and injustice. Ultimately these experiences are the touchstones to which other beliefs are referred.

Eric Voeglin first called attention to the affinities between the ancient Gnostic heresy and modern utopian poltical movements. The affinities he saw lay in the dualistic concept of the world, the saving knowledge entrusted to an elite, the meaninglessness of ordinary existence, a quasi-anarchic concept of society (later often becoming totalitarian), and the promise of total deliverance from corrupt bondage. In modern times these doctrines have been politicized, and Voeglin saw them as especially rampant in the great totalitarian movements of the twentieth century—Communism and Fascism. In the Catholic Left these political influences have melded with the cultural tendencies toward Gnosticism discussed in Chapter Five.

A legitimate question arises here—is this political Gnosticism only a phenomenon of the Catholic Left? Can it not also have its right-wing forms?

In principle the answer must be yes. Historically there have been right-wing Catholic movements which showed definite Gnostic traits, in Voeglin's sense. At the present time some aspects of the religious New Right might legitimately be seen as sharing most of those traits (except, perhaps, for antinomianism and, in most cases, mysticism). However, the New Right Christians do not at present seem to be enthusiastic in the technical sense—they think of themselves as living in fidelity to an objective authority which is biblical and to some extent ecclesiastical, rather than simply following their own inspiration. However, in practice, it seems likely that there is a good deal of Gnostic enthusiasm in the movement. It has not been discussed here because the book is primarily concerned with the Catholic Church. Although there may be a developing "New Right" there also, it is even less enthusiastic than the fundamentalist Protestants, since it tends to be faithful to traditional Catholic forms of piety and concepts of ecclesiastical authority. At present this Catholic New Right is still only incipient. Much of the public dialogue in the Church is in terms set by the Catholic Left.

Chapter 7

The Charismatic Explosion

SCARCELY anyone in 1965 would have predicted that within ten years' time the most vigorous and influential form of spiritual renewal in the Catholic Church would be a movement with strong affinities to the style and substance of Protestant pentecostalism. The Catholic charismatic movement was just beginning as the Second Vatican Council ended. By the early 1970s it was obviously one of the most vital movements around. By the mid-point of the decade it seemed possible that it would sweep the whole field of popular piety before it. By the beginning of the 1980s its dynamic growth had apparently leveled off, and there was possibly some diminution of fervor. However, it has also stabilized and become institutionalized. It would obviously be influential for a long time to come.

Virtually from the beginning, the charismatic movement was a prime candidate for criticism from the point of view of Knox's idea of enthusiasm. But a good part of that criticism was a misunderstanding —it came from people who equated enthusiasm simply with religious emotionalism. In fact, mainstream Catholicism has always made room for the welling up of strong religious emotions (in popular devotions of all kinds, for example), and there is nothing necessarily aberrant about such expressions. Some of the criticism also missed the point in simply equating a strong belief in God's actions in the world with the kind of esoteric claims advanced by the long historical parade of enthusiastic sects.[1]

Evaluation of the charismatic movement is difficult because, contrary to what might have seemed true at the beginning, it is not monolithic. Paradoxically, it has become less monolithic as it has become more institutionalized.

The difficulty of evaluation stems from the fact that, in a sense, anyone can claim to be a charismatic. If the essence of the movement is a lively sense of the Holy Spirit's actions in one's life, then anyone who possesses such an awareness is by definition a charismatic. Although most charismatics probably seek out like-minded people and participate in group activities, there is no necessity for this. In addition, what groups there are are not necessarily subject to any central discipline or uniform system of beliefs. It thus happens that virtually anything is possible under the extremely broad umbrella of the charismatic movement.

Being a charismatic is to a great extent a self-defined condition.

Toward the end of the 1970s part of the Catholic charismatic movement started to become more organized, more centralized, more consciously committed to particular doctrinal positions, more aware also of its relationship to the larger church. The paradox is that, as this was happening, other elements of the movement were, in a sense, free to go their own way, independent of that institutionalizing process and sometimes in opposition to it. Thus as the movement became more institutionalized it also began to manifest greater diversity. For purposes of analysis here it is possible to speak broadly of two wings of the move- ment, one rather closely centered on the Catholic Church, one more free-floating. For convenience's sake they can be called ecclesial charismatics and free-church charismatics respectively.[2] (The latter term is commonly used to denote those Protestant groups, like the Baptists, which emphasize the spontaneous coming together of believers rather than formal church organization.)

For yet another time, Knox's principal traits will be analyzed with reference to their contemporary applicability:[3]

Excessive piety. Always somewhat of a misnomer, the term really implies a kind of self-righteousness based on a sense of one's own superior piety. All charismatics, in one sense, practice "excessive" piety in that the intense round of private prayer, bible reading, prayer meetings, apostolic work, etc., are likely to seem extreme to Christians of average commitment. In principle, of course, it is impossible to pray too much. The point of Knox's criticism is that people of great personal piety run the risk of assuming pharisaical attitudes and of postulating their own religious superiority over others. There are cases of this, and from time to time it has seemed as though people in the charismatic movement believe that it is the only valid contemporary piety, to which all are called. As the movement comes to be more church-centered, however, it can perhaps be seen in perspective—as a powerful new form of practical piety, but not the only form.

Schism. What have been called here the ecclesial charismatics are at pains to maintain their ties to the main body of the church and to integrate their lives into the Church. There are, however, elements of the movement, what are here called free-church charismatics, who seem ecumenical in the sense of indifference to all ecclesiastical traditions. Some may overtly reject the authority of the Church. Others, however, seem merely unconcerned with it. They live in a practical state of schism in that their entire religious life revolves around prayer groups and they pay little attention to the Church as a whole. They are inclined to think that the only significant religious activity is what takes place in charismatic groups. This is the real church, the rest a distortion.

Charismatic authority. Obviously a movement which takes its name from the Spirit's bestowal of charisms, or gifts, on God's people will necessarily include a large element of charismatic authority in its makeup. The Catholic Church has always allowed for such authority, provided its scope has been limited. Founders of new religious orders, for example, usually start out in such a position—they claim divine inspiration for a task of which established authorities are often skeptical. However, they subordinate their claimed authority to that of the larger Church. This is in fact one of the tests of the authenticity of their call.

There have been problems in the charismatic movement in that it has tended to set up what may seem like parallel church structures—prayer groups or communities which substitute for parishes, community officials who seem to exercise definite authority over the members in a way analogous to the superiors of religious orders. The source of such authority has been literally charismatic—those who exercise it claim to be acting in accord with the Spirit's expressed will. It is an authority which is not answerable to or verifiable by established ecclesiastical authorities.

The free-church wing of the movement sometimes continues in this mode, although it is also less organized than the ecclesial wing. Often the free-church wing implies that established ecclesiastical authority is an obstacle to the working out of God's will in the world and that direct charismatic authority is alone valid. The ecclesial wing, much more organized, also seeks to integrate itself with the established Church structure and authority. Its authority may perhaps be seen as analogous to the authority vested in religious orders, which must always be subordinated to that of the larger Church.

Ultrasupernaturalism. The claim of direct divine inspiration is also indigenous to the charismatic movement, the workings of the Spirit in the individual soul and in the various charismatic communities. In the early years of the movement particularly, there seemed to be a considerable credulity about such inspiration—all sorts of occurrences and promptings were attributed to it. There are also charismatics, of the free-church variety, who seem impatient of every form of established authority and discipline. In classic enthusiastic fashion they listen only to what they regard as the direct promptings of the Spirit, which are often found to be in contradiction to established church authority. As noted, the ecclesial wing of the movement does seek to integrate the two.

Global pessimism. Oddly, the free-church movement, in one sense, seems to be more optimistic than the ecclesial movement, much more inclined to equate the promptings of the Spirit with the movement of history, much more likely to accept negations of traditional Christian beliefs (with regard to sexual behavior, for example). In that sense it is the opposite of global pessimism. The ecclesial wing, on the other hand, tends to share the classic Christian sense of the sinfulness of the world and particularly to be concerned about the ways in which secularistic attitudes have penetrated Christianity itself. This difference is directly related to their respective attitudes towards charismatic authority—the free-church wing, relying chiefly on what are taken to be the direct promptings of the Spirit, permits the negation of past Christian beliefs through some kind of new dispensation, while the ecclesial wing is much more respectful of scriptural authority and official Church teaching.

Anti-intellectualism. There has been a certain amount of this in the charismatic movement, especially among those who stress the Spirit's direct personal inspiration in a radical way, an inspiration which therefore largely negates the necessity of rigorous intellectual activity. There are also charismatics whose religion is so completely experiential—they cherish the intense emotion of their experiences—that they are indifferent to rigorous thought. However, the movement also has some distinguished scholars affiliated with it, and has produced some impressive works.[4]

Theocracy. Most charismatics do not seem to concern themselves with the overall organization of society. They are not political in any ordinary sense. Rather they concentrate on particular communities, sometimes implying that the believer should withdraw from the surrounding society, whch is pagan. However there is, among probably most charismatics, the belief that society should be governed in accordance with religious principles, or at least principles of basic morality.

Millenarianism. There are probably a fair number of literal millenarian beliefs among charismatics, perhaps more in the earlier stages of the movement than now. As movements of this kind mature, and become more institutionalized, millenarian expectations have a tendency to recede. They are not denied, but less emphasis is put on them. There is also a kind of millenarianism which is not a literal expectation of the end of the world but a sense rather of entering a unique time of history, in which much is demanded of believers and the challenges to faith are critical. This kind of millenarianism is fairly common among charismatics.

Mysticism. Depending on how it is defined, much of the spirituality of charismatics could be called mystical, in the sense of a direct personal experience of God in one's soul. Whether the movement has inspired mysticism in the stricter sense (as described by St. Teresa of Avila, for example) is in the nature of things unknowable.

Antinomianism. The free-church wing of the movement has certain antinomian tendencies—the promptings of the Spirit can be taken as cancelling out certain moral obligations imposed from without. The ecclesial wing, on the other hand, has been rather rigorous in upholding the objective nature of moral obligations, to which Christians must adhere. It has identified the breakdown of traditional morality as one of the chief signs of the devil's work in contemporary society.

Lust for martyrdom. To date there does not seem to be much evidence of this among charismatics, partly perhaps because there has been little opportunity for it. The ecclesial wing, at least, would emphasize the need for Christians to be willing to accept martyrdom, and the possibility that a pagan society might impose it. This is not of course the same as seeking it.

Invisible Church. The division is again between the free-church and ecclesial wings. The former does indeed seem to regard the real fellowship of believers to be spiritual, and independent of organized ecclesiastical structure. Such structure may in fact be regarded as detrimental to real Christian fellowship. The ecclesial wing, however, has recognized the importance of the visible Church and seeks to integrate itself with it.

Desire for results. Like all religious movements of any intensity, the charismatics tend to be impatient to change the world and constantly watchful for signs of God's actions there. Especially in the earlier years of the movement, there was a tendency to see all kinds of events as direct signs of that action. Any movement which is experiential naturally tends to be impatient with anything which does not bring palpable results. This is the cause of some charismatic anti-intellectualism. Some free-church charismatics continue this impatience. They are indifferent or hostile to doctrine, for example, because it does not seem to have immediate relevance. The ecclesial wing of the movement, on the other hand, as it integrates itself more into the life of the whole Church, also recognizes that God's action in the world does not always result in immediate and measurable results. A good part of every Christian's life is preparing and watching.

Experimentalism. This is, of course, close to the heart of the question, since charismatic piety is fundamentally an experiential piety. The issue at stake is to what degree the individual charismatic is willing to subordinate direct religious experience to other sources of religious authority. Some charismatics seem to regard personal experience as everything. Others, particularly in what is here called the ecclesial wing, recognize that it is not.

The famous saying of Charles Peguy, "Everything begins in *mystique* and ends up in *politique,*" has been endlessly quoted to explain the alleged corruption of historical idealistic movements, including religions. But the process by which such idealism becomes institutionalized is not merely a corruption, nor even necessarily a corruption at all. Such institutionalization is partly a necessity for survival—the values embodied in *mystique* cannot be perpetuated except in *politique*. But it is also the case that *mystique* in its pure form tends to be purely self-regarding, even solipsistic, interested in nothing except its own vision. The emergence of a *politique* is one of the principal ways in which it matures, in which it integrates its own vision with other authoritative claims. In religion the "institutional church" precisely undertakes to maintain the balance of the whole.

The charismatic movement burst upon the Church with unexpected force. As that force in some ways seems to diminish, the spirit which impelled it paradoxically makes its way to the heart of the whole Church. It can thus escape the strictures of enthusiasm.

Chapter 8

Enthusiasm's Traces

RONALD KNOX implied that enthusiasm was an isolated phenomenon, mainly found in separatist sects most of which could be dismissed as small and relatively unimportant. They had for him mainly an interest of curiosity, rather like the study of exotic pathology.

He did not foresee the possibility that, within less than two decades of the time he wrote, enthusiasm would turn out to be a pervasive religious phenomenon, important as much for its presence in the mainstream churches as in isolated sects.

For that is the important fact about contemporary religious enthusiasm. Someone has commented that the Counter-Culture of the 70s passed away only because it won most of its victories—within a few years' time the dress styles, the music, the drugs, the vocabulary, the whole panoply of what had been thought of as a radical movement had been taken over by people who were eminently respectable. The same thing happened with regard to Knox's enthusiasm. By the beginning of the 1980s its traces were everywhere. Although marginal sects, of greater or less degrees of extremism, still survived, there was, in a sense, less need for them, since the mainstream churches had almost all been affected by enthusiastic influences to one degree or another.

It is important, however, to recall exactly what the term implies. A view of religious enthusiasm which equates simply with strong emotion is misleading. All religion tends to generate strong emotion. It is also the case, perhaps more important, that some of enthusiasms's most significant manifestations are not visibly emotional. Enthusiasm is in fact most influential, and one might say most destructive, when it simply gives rise to attitudes which are habitual and unquestioned. That is what has happened to it in the present.

As has been argued here, certain social and cultural changes of the past twenty years have profoundly influenced Western Christianity, including Catholicism. These changes have been of a nature which has released what might be called the bubbles of religious enthusiasm. But even when these attitudes have lost their effervescence they have not disappeared. Instead they have insinuated themselves deeply into the main body of religion.

To begin with, it would be useful to recall the major aspects of enthusiasm as Knox delineated them, with a view to assessing their survival in the present:

Excessive piety. In one sense the opposite condition might now seem to prevail—there has been a measurable diminution of traditional pious beliefs and practices, and some Catholics are rather casually contemptuous of everything which goes under piety's name. There are, of course, exceptions to this. The charismatic movement, notably, urges its members to practice penance, to pray, to read Scripture, and in general to undertake a demanding course of religious activity. It is, however, somewhat exceptional in this regard.

Subtler but probably more relevant to Knox's meaning of enthusiasm is the attitude of religious progress, almost Gnostic in character, which was alluded to in a previous chapter. Even among people who do not claim to practice a demanding piety, and who would possibly find that concept objectionable, there is often a sense that they have broken through a higher level of religious understanding and awareness. Their notion of prayer, their approach to Scripture, their relationship to the Church, their handling of doctrine and moral precept, are all regarded, by themselves, as constituting a more mature Christianity, unfortunately not shared by the backward masses.

Schism. That schisms and sub-schisms have not taken place in the Catholic Church since the Second Vatican Council is due mainly to a policy of remarkable patience practiced by the ecclesiastical leadership, which in many cases has bent more than backwards to hold the Church together.

At the same time it can be asked if a practical state of schism does not exist in many important respects. There are groups within the Church whose doctrinal beliefs, for example, are utterly contradictory to the mainstream, and to one another. There are liturgies which quite consciously diverge, and with deliberate intent, from the official liturgy of the Church. There are individuals and groups who have, in effect, repudiated any authority the Church might have over them; their unity with the main body of the Church is nominal only. The unity of the Church is now often a merely formal thing, concealing vast and seemingly irreconcilable splits underneath.

Perhaps most important is the almost conscious tendency to schism which now exists in the Church, in the widespread celebration of "small group" manifestations of religion. Liturgies celebrated only in picked small groups, carefully selected prayer groups, small communities selected out from within larger religious orders, worshipping communities formed of people who have deliberately rejected membership in a parish—all these seem to serve the purpose of permitting a kind of religious affiliation which bypasses the main body of the Church, which is centered on special communities. In time some of these groups become formally schismatic. Avant-garde Catholic thought now extols this kind of separateness and correspondingly denigrates the importance of membership in the larger Church.

Charismatic authority. The nature of this authority should not be equated with the kind of authority which exists in the so-called charismatic movement, although it does sometimes exist there. It is something broader in character as Knox understands it, referring to those who claim religious leadership by virtue of special divine inspiration independent of established ecclesiastical structures.

The manifestations of charismatic authority in the contemporary Church are legion. At various times it has been claimed by liturgical innovators, theologians, reformers of religious orders, political activists, and numerous other categories of persons. The Catholic Church allows for possible direct divine inspiration of individuals in extraordinary circumstances. This is, perhaps in essence, what sainthood is. The crucial point is the relationship of claimed charismatic authority to established ecclesiastical authority. The history of the Church is littered with instances of people who claimed such authority but whose claim the considered judgment of the Church finally disallowed. In the present Church such claims are practically epidemic—the ease with which would-be innovators profess a special divine charism makes practically every third Catholic a proclaimed prophet. In most instances this kind of authority is consciously set in opposition to established ecclesiastical authority, and the claim is made that those who hold Church office have somehow lost their authority, which has passed to some challenger.

Ultrasupernaturalism. Again, in a literal sense, this seems perhaps less prevalent than it may once have been. There is in the contemporary Church, if anything, an excess of skepticism about all things supernatural, a sometimes unexamined conviction that a sophisticated worldliness explains those things which the credulous attribute to divine intervention.

In another sense, a sense analogous to charismatic authority as outlined above, this phenomenon can be seen still to exist, albeit in a less obvious form. It resides now in the tendency to see the hand of God in all kinds of worldly movements—political, social, intellectual, cultural—so that the duty of the believer is said to be to support these movements, which manifest the will of God. There is present here a naivete about divine action which is just as simplistic as that which traditional piety sometimes encouraged.

Global pessimism. As noted before, officially the religiosity of the past twenty years is optimistic. It holds the world and all that is in it to be good, and as a result often cannot see the need for forgiveness and salvation. However, this official optimism often cloaks an actual pessmism, as also argued before. In particular is this manifest in certain kinds of radical political activism claiming Christian inspiration, an activism which feels compelled to condemn "the system" in global terms and to perceive the social order, if not the individual, as in need of total redemption.

Anti-intellectualism. Superficially this may again seem inapplicable to the present Church, where the assault on traditional beliefs and practices has gone forward under the banner of scholarship and creative thought. But there can be no denying that much of what passes for thought in the contemporary Church —in liturgy, in social and political affairs, in morals—is shoddy and heavily dependent on cultural fads. Often overlooked is the degree to which the anti-dogmatic impulse is itself inherently anti-intellectual. The Catholic tradition has lavished immense care, subtlety, and intellectual effort on the expression and elaboration of Catholic beliefs, a process which has attracted the best minds of the Church for nearly two millenia. Now this whole dogmatic heritage is often implicitly dismissed as irrelevant.

Religious education in recent years has, paradoxically, often sought to teach people less about their faith rather than more. The assumption holds sway that formal intellectual understanding of faith is necessarily sterile. Contrasted to it is an approach to religion which sees it as a highly personal, even subjective experience. Knowledge of faith is deemed unimportant so long as the proper attitudes are imbibed.

Theocracy. Again the highly secularized modern Christian may seem a long way from the dangers of theocracy. But this is true only in the most literal sense of the term. The secularization of the contemporary Christian mind has precisely created the conditions which make a messianic politics possible. What has been notable in many contemporary socially minded Christians is their lack of patience with ordinary parliamentary democracy, for example, their constant searching for a messianic regime, often Marxist in character, which will embody the Kingdom of God on earth.

Millenarianism. There has been some literal millenarianism in contemporary Christianity, in the sense of an expectation of the imminent Second Coming of Christ. More important, however, has been the resurgence of what is sometimes called "realized eschatology," that is, a loss of interest in, even perhaps a rejection of, the idea of the Kingdom of God as eternal, following upon the end of the world, in favor of the belief that the Kingdom of God will be realized on this earth. Again, the contemporary Christian is likely to give this an essentially political and secular meaning.

Mysticism. As noted, the 1970s in America turned out to be a religious tropical jungle, and one important aspect of this was a revival of interest in mysticism. Rarely noticed, however, was the fact that the Catholic Church does not believe in mysticism in general. In fact an important part of the writings of the great Catholic mystics, notably St. Teresa of Avila, are taken up with warnings about false mysticism and false manifestations of mysticism. However, the rediscovery of mysticism in the 1970s was nothing if not indiscriminate—the mystical experience was treated as a goal in and of itself, and the very possibility of discriminating between true and false mysticism was often denied.[1]

Antinomianism. The antinomian attitude—the assertion that through faith one is freed from the need for obedience to the law—is almost pandemic in modern Christianity, largely as a result of the social and cultural breakdown discussed in previous chapters. There are complex reasons for this attitude. One of the most important, however, is a distorted notion of faith, whereby if one has faith in God one is accepted as he is and one's moral behavior is not judged. There is a kind of reverse pharisaism involved—the believer openly deviates from the law in order to show his liberation from the narrow concept of Christianity which characterizes the unenlightened church member.

Lust for martyrdom. As noted in connection with Gnosticism, this is perhaps the major tenet of historical enthusiasm which does not apply to contemporary Christianity. At the same time, the history of Gnosticism also seems to show that Knox was mistaken in seeing this as an essential quality of enthusiasm. Only in a political context does the desire for martyrdom have much legitimacy for the contemporary avant-garde Christian.

Invisible Church. Following the Second Vatican Council it became almost routine to contrast the merely "institutional Church" with the (presumably) true Church. The latter was made up of those who truly believed and who often found themselves at odds with or alienated from the visible Church. Such an attitude is now widespread and is closely related to the phenomenon of schism discussed above.

Desire for results. Knox saw this as applying mainly to what might be called spiritual results—the open and palapable manifestation of God's work in one's life. Contemporary Christianity provides numerous examples of this expectation. However, in the essentially secularized form which all these things now take, the present manifestation of it is somewhat different. Perhaps most important is the widespread belief that religion, in order to be valid, must prove its social usefulness. Certain very basic religious concepts, like that of worship, are now under a cloud because they do not appear to have measurable effect on the world. The principal purpose of human society is more and more understood as that of remaking the world, and whatever does not fit this purpose is ruthlessly cast aside.

Experimentalism. The previously noted desire for results obviously fits this last of Knox's major qualities, that which places final and ultimate emphasis on intense and personal religious experiences. This attitude too is now all but pervasive in Christianity. The cultivation of intense and subjective personal religious experiences is a major preoccupation, and such experiences alone are thought to have enduring validity. This is the opposite side of the coin of anti-intellectualism.

Notice should also be taken of certain other characteristics of historical enthusiasm as Knox found them. These are qualities which he did not identify as principal defining traits but which he did mention in passing as recurring features of enthusiasm as he studied it. These, too, seem to have considerable contemporary relevance:

Separation of Christ and his Church. Knox found that enthusiasts usually had so intense a sense of their own personal relationship to Christ, of God's direct intervention in their lives, that they found the Church more of a obstacle to their relationship to him than a help. Obviously this is directly related to the primarily invisible understanding of Church noted previously. This kind of anti-ecclesiastical Christianity is fairly common now even among Catholics. An interesting variant on it is purely secularistic—the appropriation of Christ by non-believers, with the corresponding insistence that the Church has somehow distorted or obscured Christ's real teachings. The popular musical *Jesus Christ Superstar* is a significant example.

Liturgical deviation. Knox used the term "liturgical decency" to designate the positive quality which he found enthusiasts rejecting—the sense of correctnesses, of observance of the law, of decorum, and proportion. In 1950 these were things which were automatically thought of as characteristic of Catholic worship.

Correlatively, as Knox also noted, there is a seemingly irresistible historical impulse for people of enthusiastic persuasion to dismiss liturgical rules and established rituals as merely bothersome or stultifying. So intense is their emphasis on themselves and their own experiences that they demand the right to engage in purely personal and expressive worship. Liturgical rules are considered at best appropriate for the unenlightened masses but not to the religious elite. Assertions of the "right" to liturgical experimentation has, of course, been one of the principal features of Catholic life since the Second Vatican Council.

Feminism. Knox's keen eye noticed how often in history enthusiastic movements have been accompanied by a kind of religious feminism, in which women have played roles equal to men in the life of the sects, have functioned as preachers, prophets, or other spiritual leaders. He connected this to the enthusiastic element itself—the single-minded emphasis on direct divine inspiration, so that women who felt such inspiration were immediately justified in coming forward.

The same feminist element has also been noticed in

connection with Gnosticism, and it has been discussed in connection with Mary Douglas' theories of the relationship between ritual and society. This point about religious feminism has important relevance to the situation today, which Knox did not foresee— apart from the abstract question whether women can or should function as clergy, ecclesiastical feminism always functions as an attack on the traditional ecclesiastical order. It pits direct inspiration against hierarchical authority in a specially forceful way. It is thus virtually impossible to reconcile with authentic historical Catholicism.

Denial of infant baptism. Knox also noticed this as a recurring historical phenomenon—among the Donatists of St. Augustine's time, for example, and especially among the Anabaptists of the Reformation period. The principal argument against infant baptism has been a strong emphasis on direct personal inspiration. Infants should not be baptized because they are merely passive recipients of the sacrament. Only those should be baptized who feel a direct and special call to do so. Implicitly, the rejection of infant baptism is a rejection of the Catholic understanding of the sacraments.

Although there has not been a systematic attack on the practice of infant baptism in recent years, it is a subject which has been fairly widely discussed. Avant-garde liturgists sometimes express embarrassment over the practice.

Priestly unworthiness. Few points in the history of the Church have occasioned more heated and sensitive discussion than the matter of a priest's personal worthiness in relationship to the exercise of his office. Certain heresies have been strongly condemned by the Church for their insistence that a sinful priest loses his priestly authority. With their strong emphasis on direct personal inspiration, the enthusiastic sects inevitably took the same position.

The issue has not arisen in recent times in precisely this way. Indeed the present tendency is to excuse everyone's moral failings amidst a sea of amorphous good will. However, the notion that priestly ordination automatically confers sacramental power on a man is one which has fallen under a cloud, and there is a growing tendency to see the priest in essentially Protestant terms, as someone who discharges a social office.

New liturgical styles have given emphasis to the priest's personal qualities as never before in the Church's history. Many people search carefully for the "right" priest whom they regard as capable of officiating at the Eucharist. There is much talk of certain people (not necessarily priests) having the "qualities of celebrants" and of these people therefore being qualified to officiate at the Mass. More and more, liturgy comes to seem a projection of the celebrant's own personality.

To reiterate what was said in connection with the discussion of Gnosticism, if one feature of modern religious enthusiasm could be singled out as crucial it would be the denial of the genuinely historical character of religion, which involves therefore a denial of the essential nature of Christianity itself. Even further, it involves a denial of the essential nature of Catholicism, because Catholicism is perhaps the most unabashedly historical of any religion in the world.

A key manifestation of this mentality is the sense that the past of the Church is largely a burden, alternately oppressive, embarrassing, irrelevant, and meaningless. Much time and energy are spent throwing off this burden. A good deal of what passes for scholarship, for example, is in the debunking mode, aimed at somehow discrediting the past. (This is an operation which extends sometimes even to Scripture.) Religious education is deliberately restructured to eliminate the past—historic creeds, stories of the saints, traditional liturgical forms, and many other things which go to make up the Church's living tradition are effectively censored.[2]

In these terms the believer's relationship to the past is purely one of liberation—the ability to discard the authority of the past brings with it a sense of freedom and exhilaration—Mary Douglas' effervescence. After a time the past is successfully filtered out of one's consciousness. However, it remains always a vague threat, a possible atavism. The suitably "renewed" Christian develops automatic defense mechanisms for warding off even the remote threat of the power of the past invading the present. There is a sometimes fanatical insistence on a wholly contemporary style in dress, liturgy, music, verbal expression, and a host of other things which serve to surround the individual with a modern idiom.

This mentality, which is at the very root of enthusiasm, cannot conceive the possibility of organic growth from the past. The idea of such growth is indeed extolled. Cardinal Newman's postulate of the development of doctrine is ritualistically invoked, but usually without any effort to understand what Newman meant by it. What is termed organic development is, increasingly, simply the negation of the past—in morality, in doctrine, in lifestyle. History goes dead.

The loss of history proceeds in certain fairly predictable stages as far as the Catholic Church is concerned, and a key to understanding them lies in an understanding of the word "reform." The word means, of course, literally "to form again." It means the recovery of the original nature of something which has been lost. It implies historical deformation, a process of change whereby the purity of the original vision has been lost.

Thus reformers in the history of the Church have always been people seeking to return to an original vision. They have, contrary to the modern understanding of the term, not been future-oriented but past-oriented in some ultimate sense. However, there is one crucial difference between authentically Catholic reformers and those who have merely appropriated the name—Catholic reformers seek to return to an original purity while also allowing for organic development or tradition. The Protestant spirit of reform is one which negates all the intervening centuries since the beginning and seeks to return literally to a pure early church. The conflict over Tradition is at the root of the historic Catholic-Protestant split.

But there is an odd paradox here. Those reformers who repudiate all of history in order to return to the pure original sources end up demythologizing the sources themselves. It is no accident that Protestantism, which began by insisting on *sola Scriptura,* the Bible alone as the rule of faith, was also first to admit those theories of modern philosophy and exegesis which discredit the historical reliability of Scripture. For the reforming mentality in this sense is profoundly hostile to history, can find in it no meaning. Thus the Scriptures also must be taken out of history.

The same path has been followed by reform-minded Catholics since the Second Vatican Council. At first renewal called forth a new interest and veneration of the Scripture. Its true test, however, was whether it could integrate that veneration with an authentically Catholic veneration for Tradition. All too soon it became obvious that this would not happen. It is now routine in Catholic circles to juxtapose Scripture and Church tradition in contradictory ways. The Protestant practice of using Scripture to discredit the Church, to judge the Church and find it wanting, is now so deeply ingrained in many Catholics that they do it instinctively and without conscious reflection.

However, it was inevitable that once this happened Catholic veneration for Scripture could not survive, any more than it survived in modern Protestantism. Within about ten years' time the Catholic Church had recapitulated the 400-year history of Protestantism, down to and including the discrediting of the historicity of Scripture.

Both modern Protestants and modern Catholics profess indignantly that their questioning of the historicity of Scripture does not in any way involve a lessening of their veneration of it or their acceptance of its authority. The point, however, is that once the historicity of Scripture is undermined, even if only partially, its interpretation becomes wholly open, its meaning more and more subjective. One can profess respect for the teaching authority of Scripture, but that authority more and more becomes a reflection of one's own concerns. Scripture is more and more like a mirror in which one descries the outline of one's own countenance.

The key here is the understanding which is given to the concept of historicity itself. Rather than understanding it as it is used here, as the fact of being situated in history and therefore as part of its ongoing development, the contemporary mind tends to understand it in the sense of what is often called historicism. It is actually using history to escape from

history, by positing that each age is so unique, so
culturally and temporaly circumscribed, that meaningful links between one age and another become virtually impossible. With regard to both Scripture and
Church tradition, this means that the creations of the
past are dismissed as necessarily irrelevant to the present. Scripture is treated as the creation of the Hel-
lenistic Middle Eastern world of the first century
A.D. Thus its message is essentially time-bound, and
later Christians are free to adjust, adapt, even censor
that message to suit the needs of their own time.

No concern has exercised greater power over the
contemporary Christian mind than the search for
community. People have gone to obsessive lengths—
in liturgy, in church structure, in the use of therapeutic techniques—to find this elusive reality. Yet
it has remained elusive, paradoxically contributing
mightily to the sectarian fragmentation of the churches, as people find traces of community only in highly
specialized groups very much like themselves.

True community in the Christian sense is the Communion of the Saints, which involves the unity of all
believers living and dead, the great democracy of all
those who have gone before with the sign of faith and
who sleep the sleep of peace. The "old liturgy" was
premised precisely on this unity, and this was the
community it created. It was the widest possible community, based on the common history shared by all.
Newer understandings both of community and of liturgy end by losing the sense of community because

they progressively narrow it and restrict it. Lacking a common and very deep history, people find no basis for community except in ephemeral subjective experience. Thus enthusiastic groups always manifest characteristics of narrow sectarianism and of emotional and highly subjective piety, both aimed at the receding possibility of community.

The tendency of enthusiastic sects to split and resplit is also not accidental. Their bases of community are so fragile and subjective as to be easily shattered. Precisely because they lack a strong and deep common history, they cannot withstand shocks and strains. There is the inevitable tendency to draw the circle narrower and narrower, to achieve community by systematically shutting out whatever threatens to upset the very delicate balance of subjective factors which make a sense of community possible. Perhaps the most poignant test case in recent years has been in Catholic religious orders which, as they progressively lost contact with their own living traditions, found themselves splitting in a dozen different ways and large numbers of their members breaking with the community completely, returning to the lay state. These visibly fragmented and divided communities then attracted few new members.

The new religiosity sometimes presents itself as future-oriented. However, this usually proves to be mere wishfulness, since no one can know the future. Avant-garde religious continually project what they think the future holds and attempt to adjust present religion accordingly. But they are continually surprised by history, a surprise which forces the discarding of all their well-laid plans. The very religious revival of the 1970s was, as noted, an immense surprise to the secularizers of the 1960s. Religious communities carefully "renewed" to make them relevant to the present find themselves attracting few people, even as traditional communities continue to do so.

Rather than future-orientation, what the new religiosity offers instead is a perspective which is wholly concentrated on the present. It cannot find either a meaningful past or a discernible future. An elusive and sometimes desperately thin grasp on the present is all it has. What it seeks is an eternal present. But this too remains unattainable for, as Mary Douglas points out, the destruction both of community and of a meaningful past frees the individual, but only for life in a present which is chaotic and meaningless. It give rise to unchecked egotism, to social hostilities, to moral and intellectual confusion.

Chapter 9

Conclusion

THE rejection of an historical faith in favor of an eternal present is at the root of religious enthusiasm for a very important reason—the rejection of history turns religion into a wholly subjective phenomenon which exists largely at the will of the individual. Historicity imparts to social phenomena specific and fixed identities. The Church might have developed in some other way than it did (for example, in the Gnostic way), but in fact it did not. The refusal to accept these "givens" of history is the essence of the enthusiastic position.

Enthusiasm almost always represents itself as more intense, more pious, and more demanding than conventional faith, which by contrast often seems dull, routinized, and comfortable. In intention many of its adherents do indeed seek a more genuine and profound faith. However, having cut itself off from its historical roots it inevitably falls into certain traps which become progressively more ensnaring.

The crucial claim of the enthusiasts is that they experience God in their lives in a direct and powerful way, more direct and more powerful than the ordinary channels of religion provide. For some people, at least, the claim may be true.

Enthusiasm then goes on to promise that this powerful experience of the divine will be permanent and, furthermore, that it is necessary. Rather than merely saying that certain personal experiences of God are more intense than those achieved through the Church, enthusiasm begins to posit almost a direct conflict between the two—the closer one remains to the "institutional church," the further one is likely to be from God.

The problem of enthusiasm, in the end, is that it has no way of validating religious experiences. Ecclesiastical authority, and the traditions which it embodies, has been rejected out of hand. Scripture remains. But, as already noted, once Scripture loses its historicity, it too becomes non-authoritative. It functions more and more as the subjective extension of the present. It can be made to yield up whatever teachings the contemporary mind wants to find there.

Finally, intense experience simply comes to be equated with the divine. Since no means exists whereby experiences might be discriminated, all experiences can be called divine if the individual chooses to do so. The search for intense experience comes to be self-validating. Experience is its own justification.

Eventually, for the enthusiast, nothing any longer has any meaning except one's own personal experiences. The external world comes to seem less and less real. The self expands more and more to fill the space of the universe.

In religious terms this is explained by saying that all religious belief rests on personal experience, a formula which excludes the possibility of genuine revelation. But the growing tendency to pronounce all experience as divine or of divine origin soon gives rise to a concept of God which is really equatable with the self at the deepest level. One's own impulses are interpreted as God's will, the stirrings of one's own psyche as God manifesting himself. The search for self through therapeutic means, for example, is announced as a search for God.

It is a mistake to think of enthusiasm as confined to bizarre sects, as Knox essentially saw it. As has been argued here, it is found in many different forms and in today's Christianity is almost pervasive. Nor is it equatable simply with religious emotionalism. Devotees of a radical social gospel, for example, eschew most familiar forms of that emotionalism but at the same time show certain enthusiastic tendencies. The charismatic movement has been most commonly cited as the leading contemporary example of enthusiasm, but in certain ways it has sought to counteract those tendencies, especially in positing an objective moral order and necessary ecclesiastical structure.

As has been argued here, there has been an immense resurgence of enthusiasm in the past twenty years largely because of social and cultural changes. It has had deleterious affects on genuine Christianity but has also provided the means for at least potential religious revivals. If on the whole it has persuaded people to worship themselves and call that self God, it has perhaps also provided them with the tools of religious awareness which in time will enable them to rediscover the God of Abraham, of Isaac, and of Jacob.

Notes

CHAPTER ONE

1. *Enthusiasm, A Chapter in the History of Religion, with Special Reference to the XVII and XVIII Centuries* (New York: Oxford University Press, 1950).

2. The authorized biography of Knox is by his friend Evelyn Waugh—*Msgr. Ronald Knox* (London, 1959).

3. Waugh, *The Diaries of Evelyn Waugh,* ed. Michael Davie (Boston, 1976), p. 296.

4. Norman Ravitch in the *American Historical Review,* Oct., 1975, p. 961.

5. The most noted (and controversial) study of Gnosticism in its Christian context is Elaine Pagels, *The Gnostic Gospels* (New York, 1979). See also Hans Jonas, *The Gnostic Religion* (Boston, 1958).

6. Gordon Leff, *Heresy in the Later Middle Ages* (Manchester, England, 1967), two volumes.

7. John S. Oyer, *Lutherans against Anabaptists* (The Hague, Netherlands, 1964).

CHAPTER TWO

1. For a discussion of this in the context of the late Roman Empire see E. R. Dodds, *Pagan and Christian in an Age of Anxiety* (Cambridge, England, 1965).

2. These were the theories of Margaret Murray, *The God of the Witches* (London, 1933) and *The Witch Cult in Western Europe* (Oxford, 1921).

3. Richard Woods, O.P., *The Occult Revolution* (New York, 1971).

4. For a critique of humanistic psychology from a Christian perspective see Paul Vitz, *Psychology as Religion* (Grand Rapids, Mich., 1978).

5. For a discussion of this from a liberal Protestant viewpoint see Dean M. Kelley, *Why the Conservative Churches Are Growing* (New York, 1973).

CHAPTER THREE

1. The term is from a book of that title by the literary critic Quentin Anderson—*The Imperial Self* (New York, 1971). For a more thorough discussion of the subject in a religious context see the chapter with the same title in Hitchcock, *Catholicism and Modernity* (New York, 1979).

2. *The Seduction of the Spirit—People's Religion in the 1970s* (New York, 1973).

CHAPTER FOUR

1. *Natural Symbols* (New York, 1970).

2. For a discussion of Catholic liturgical change, using Mary Douglas's categories of analysis, see Hitchcock, *The Recovery of the Sacred* (New York, 1974).

3. See Landon Y. Jones, *Great Expectations* (New York, 1980).

CHAPTER FIVE

1. Hans Jonas, *The Gnostic Religion* (Boston, 1958).
2. *The Gnostic Gospels* (New York, 1979).
3. Daniel Berrigan and Robert Coles, *The Geography of Faith* (Boston, 1971), p. 79.

CHAPTER SIX

1. *The New Science of Politics* (Chicago: 1972), pp. 123-4, 129, 131.
2. See for example an interview in *Salt,* February, 1981, p. 3.
3. For a discussion of the Catholic Left's affinity for totalitarianism see Hitchcock, *Catholicism and Modernity,* Ch. 7, "The Road to Utopia."
4. See for example Matthew Fox, O.P., *On Becoming a Musical, Mystical Bear* (New York, 1972).
5. *National Catholic Reporter,* June 8, 1973, p. 1.
6. *Commonweal,* Oct. 17, 1981, pp. 65; *National Catholic Reporter,* Dec. 17, 1971, p. 4.

CHAPTER SEVEN

1. See for example Kieran Quinn, "Knox, Me, and the Pentecostals," *National Catholic Reporter,* Nov. 9, 1973, pp. 7-8.
2. What is here called the ecclesial wing of the movement is centered around the journal *New Covenant.* The so-called free-church wing is less easily identified, precisely because it is diffuse and not centralized. A representative figure would be the famous healer Francis McNutt, O.P., who left the priesthood and married in 1979.
3. For a further discussion of these issues, with an attempt at a balanced evaluation of the movement, see Hitchcock and Sr. Gloriana Bednarski, R.S.M., *Catholic Perspectives: Charismatics* (Chicago: Thomas More Association, 1980).

4. For example see Stephen Clark, *Man and Woman in Christ* (Ann Arbor, Mich., 1980). The work brings together an impressive array of data and insights from a wide variety of intellectual disciplines.

CHAPTER EIGHT

1. For example, Fox, *On Becoming a Musical Mystical Bear.*

2. For a further discussion of this see the chapters entitled "The Loss of History" in two books by the author—*The Recovery of the Sacred* (New York, 1974) and *Catholicism and Modernity* (New York, 1978).